MW01106054

Meditations, Mediums, and Manna

(for those with co-occurring disorders)

Scott L. Gourson PhD

Meditations, Mediums, and Manna

This book of meditations, mediums, and manna is for all those who struggle with this journey between mental health issues, substance use, and sanity. Know that we can emerge into Recovery and have happy, joyful, and free lives.

Preface

I should explain the title. Meditations: things to ponder. Mediums: vehicles for spiritual development. And manna: spiritual sustenance. It is my hope this volume provides each of these things.

It is for the dually diagnosed individual; those with substance use issues and other mental health matters. You are close to my heart. I believe the spiritual piece is essential for Recovery. Meditations, Mediums, and Manna is based on AA premises, Person-Centered Theory, Existential Philosophy, and Kabalistic principles.

Table of Contents

Worry

Thought

Hah! Worry. Do you worry? I bet you do! Do you worry about just certain things or do you worry about every-thing…regardless? My psychiatrist used to tell me I was an 'oi vey kind of guy'!

Funny thing was, I had a harder time with the little stuff. You know, what brand of toothpaste do I want this time or, geez, I didn't pick up my socks….they were still on the floor…that had the potential to nag at me.

I learned to separate out what was a legitimate worry and what was OCD worry and I learned to give myself permission to let go of the OCD stuff. Whew! We really can gain some control over this stuff.

Medication can help with these things too. It's not terrible.

Has worry ever been productive for you? I used to think my 'concern' kept me focused. Well, maybe it did. But perhaps there are other ways to remain focused?

Resolution

Things will be ok whether I worry about them or not. When I involve my Higher Power in my life, I can be confident that it is all-good and all will be well. What would happen if I stopped worrying today? I'd be free to be happy and enjoy the day!

Faith

Thought

Faith. Faith. Faith, such a calm and relaxing feeling. Such a quietness of spirit. Faith is a practical matter; it is a very pragmatic tool. Everything will be all right! It is fundamental. How we think it, is how it is. We have a choice in how we are going to look upon things. But it doesn't feel like it, huh?

When we are in the throes of addiction or in the mire of depression, it doesn't feel like anything else is possible. When we attend meetings, we get to see other people emerging from their depths of despair. It is easier to see progress in other people than in us. It gives us hope that maybe we, too, can get better. We begin to believe it. As time goes on, we get to count on it.

Resolution

I will make faith a cornerstone in my recovery today. I will remember that what I think and believe today paves the road for tomorrow. Things do not improve unless I believe that they can!

Freedom

Thought

When we are using, we are prisoners of our addiction. We are limited by the confines of our own thinking. This is why we need a power greater than ourselves. We need someone to release the shackles. This is the nature of recovery from addiction. We cannot do it alone. Our addiction is a Force that will continue to keep us bound up within its confines. It will continue to put us in the exact position we need to keep on using. It will create just the right situations with just the right people in just the right places for us to continue using. Our addiction is bigger than we are. On our own, we are limited by our thinking to get out from under.

Resolution

Freedom from my addiction begins when I look outside of myself for answers. Today I will allow myself to include others in my recovery. I am learning to understand today, that being open to a power greater than myself spawns my independence.

Letting Go

Thought

I was always possessed and preoccupied by thinking about, worrying about, and obsessing about one thing or another. There was always some lingering upset waiting to be resolved. I couldn't even enjoy when something did resolve before being bombarded with the next thing.

One day it dawned on me that the problem was not any one of these singular issues, situations, conflicts, problems, feelings, thoughts, fears, worries, and so on and so forth...the problem was simply my anxiety itself! I kept looking for one solution after another for this issue and that. It was endless. Endless. The anxiety affected me in so many different ways; from stress to esteem to productivity. My doctor and I found a medication that helped a lot.

I have the ability to let go today. It is among my most precious gifts received. I am able to recognize when my worry is out of concern or obsession. Concerns I deal with. Obsessions I let go.

Resolution

Does my condition warrant the anxiety or depression that I feel? Or is my condition manufactured by my anxiety or depression? Today I will discern between conditions that can be dealt with and those that need to be let go.

Doubt

Thought

Anything I used to think about – task, feeling, desire, what have you – was always underscored by feelings of doubt. Do you question yourself? Do you question your ability to do a job, go to school, and enter a relationship? D o you ever steer clear of something because you don't think it possible or that you cannot succeed or will not accomplish it? Do you doubt that circumstances will favor you? How much does doubt hold you back? What forms does it take?

In my Saturday morning peripatetic AA meeting, we often discuss our common "less than syndrome". We have all shared how we never felt good enough, never fit in, were never right, were always wrong, distinguished by feelings of inadequacy, and marked by despair.

Doubt is destructive. It tears us down. Prevents us from doing so many things. It keeps us in a perpetual state of need.

Resolution. I am learning today how much doubt plays a part in all that I do. I have no room… for doubt… in my life in recovery. I am moving forward in my thinking in a positive and productive manner. I shall have a deaf ear to the laments of doubt.

Happy, Joyous, and Free

Thought

Early on in my recovery, I heard the expression *"happy, joyous, and free"* batted about. People claimed to be "happy, joyous and free". Was this true? Was this possible? People seemed to think that believed that our Higher Power wanted us to be.....happy, joyous, and free! It sounded very lofty. How could I ever get out from under my anxiety and shame?

Well, there are some essential ingredients. It begins with Trust. Steadfast trust. Steadfast trust in a Higher Power. Steadfast trust in a Higher Power that all will be well. This involves a leap of faith.

Let me ask you a question. At this stage in the game, what have you got to lose? All will be well and it will be well in a real and palpable way.

One must talk with their Higher Power. One must exercise everything in their power for a positive outcome. One must always, always....maintain hope. Regardless how powers to be seem to prevail and the situation remains unchanged, one must be firm in his trust that through prayer, perseverance, and continuing to do the next right thing that the situation can be entirely reversed beyond one's realm of possibility.

One continues to ask for sustenance, health, as well as all their needs. If unfavorable conditions present themselves, he is grateful. Yes. He is grateful for his blessings and for the opposite as well. Joyfully.

What!? Let me clarify. Whatever occurs, is for our good. Yes. And this, too, is good. It is not for loss, but will prove to be a gain.

Provisionally, living in the fashion described, provides energy, enthusiasm and joy. And one is, discernibly and fundamentally, *alive*. No matter what changes in one's life, nothing can take away from his *life force* and subsequent ability to accept his situation happily. At the same time, one asks and trusts that his circumstances change in a positive, real, and palpable way.

Resolution

I will allow joy to permeate my life. I recognize that focusing on my unhappiness and woes only keeps me submerged in mire. I will live my recovery in joy because it provides me with the power, strength, and energy to overcome anything in my path.

Joy

Thought

Recovery must be lived in Joy. Joy is a powerful thing. When we are joyful, we feel security, clarity, faith, trust, and love. It provides us with the ability to move through our day in an easy and relaxed way.

Depression and sadness are its' opposite. They weigh us down and make us heavy, slow, and impotent. We must fight against it to the best of our ability. We recognize that we have medical (psychiatric) needs as well as spiritual needs. Some of us benefit from medication. We can have a medication awakening. This can allow us to have a spiritual awakening.

We must first feel our feelings, accept them, *and then let them go.* Anytime we engage in depression or anxiety, we are nourishing our negative forces. This is a useless and destructive process. One thought begets another.

Analyzing our feelings and thoughts may also be counterproductive. If analyzing serves to prevent us from making the same mistake again, it is positive. But it must be done in a *joyful* way. If our analyzing just serves to makes us feel worse about ourselves, or if the process is a painful one, it does not serve us well.

Much of the time, we can *choose* the course of our thinking. We cannot control what comes into our head, but can certainly determine what we harbor and dwell on.

Recovery calls for us to live in a joyful way. If something is preventing our joy in life, such as our depression, sadness, or analyzing, we must move away from it. Much of the time, we can *direct* our thoughts in a positive direction.

Resolution

I know that Recovery is about bringing joy to life. Joy is not the *result* of positive and wonderful things in our life: Joy is the *cause* of positive and wonderful things in our life. I will take care of both my psychiatric and spiritual needs today. I will not allow sadness, depression, or futile, analyzing to permeate my space. I know that I cannot control thoughts that come into my head, but I know that much of the time, I can *choose* the direction of my thinking.

Struggle

Thought

Struggle is inherent in life. We are always struggling and *should be.* Even if we are happy, joyous, and free, we continue to push ourselves to improve further. Most of us wonder if the struggle will ever be over. Do we ever reach a point where struggling stops? We think, "am I going to be 95 and still going to meetings?" "Isn't the cake ever baked and ready to come out of the oven?" my friend Phylss would say.

Our purpose in life is our soul's growth. And a large part of our soul's growth is about mastering ourselves. Mastering ourselves means harnessing our negative energy. We are always struggling with this on one level or another. Our level of behavior yesterday no longer meets our level of growth today. We continue to refine ourselves.

Our refinement is directly related to our relationship with our Higher Power. We need our Higher Power to help us overcome our obsession to drink/drug. We need a Higher Power because the obsession to use is bigger than we are. We need the direction and guidance to overcome our other mental health issues. We manage to meet the right people in the right places to help us do the right things for our recovery. This is Providence.

But we must choose to reach up and then listen to the guidance we need in order to have the power to carry out the directions we receive. The purpose of the trials and tribulations of our struggle is to bring us closer to our Higher Power.

Resolution

I understand that struggle is a necessary part of life and that it brings me closer to my Higher Power. Today I will connect with and enrich my relationship with my Higher Power. My relationship with a Higher Power is its' own reward. Today I listen to the guidance and direction that I receive. I revel in His presence and am grateful for that which brings me closer to Him. I strive for conscious contact with my Higher Power. It is the most important thing that I possess because it supercedes all other matters and helps me rise above the material concerns of my struggle.

Forces

Thought

Remember when you were a kid and your parents told you that God wrote down everything that you did in the *Good Book* and the *Bad Book* and that you had an angel on one shoulder and the devil on the other?

Well, that's not far from the truth. For our purposes, there are two Forces at play here: your Addiction and your Recovery. It is important to personify them because they have distinct personalities. Either we are moving forward in our Recovery or backwards to our Addiction. There is *no* standing still.

Anything that enhances our lives in a positive and joyful way is our Recovery talking. Everything else is your Addiction talking. Your Recovery knows just what you need and provides us with direction, guidance and the power to carry them out. It brings you to the Right people at the Right time for the Right things.

Your Addiction knows you very well also. And it knows just what conditions, circumstances, thoughts and feelings will send you back out there. It too, will put you with the right people in the right places to get you high.

Who are you going to listen to? Right. It's not always that simple. You will learn to know instinctively who is talking. Meetings, sponsors, and your other friends in recovery can help you figure it out if you are in question. It's amazing how the Voice of AA will keep us on the Right path.

The question to ask oneself when trying to make a decision *and determine whose talking* is: Does this (the situation at hand) ultimately lead me back to Addiction or forward in my Recovery? Often, the answer is clear. Often, if we hesitate to answer, that may tell us something. If we are in doubt, have a reservation, or are hesitating, there is a reason for it

Resolution

I recognize that there are powerful Forces at play here. And I know that as long as I do the Right thing, and then the next Right thing, I have nothing to fear. I am going to listen to my voice of Recovery. If I'm ever in doubt, I know that I can ask people in the fellowship. They say that Addiction is cunning, baffling, and powerful. I must not underestimate it. While I'm laying the foundation for my Recovery, my Addiction is out there doing push-ups. I know that it has the ability to pull the wool over my eyes. That's why I need a Power greater than myself and to surround myself with people in the fellowship.

Presence

Thought

The pain and suffering of our addiction serves to bring us closer to our Higher Power. When we have moved along in our spiritual development, we come to realize that this is why we went through all of that misery. We were broken people. It is when we are genuinely broken that we try to establish contact with our Higher Power. We need to be broken so that there is nothing else left that we can do – but to reach out to Him. And we reach.....with our whole being......our heart, soul, and mind. This is what it takes. It takes the need to have to reach with our whole being before we have an appreciation for God's Presence in our life.

You see, our Higher Power needed to get our attention. Everything we endured was for a High and Mighty Purpose. Do you see that? Now we are aware that a Higher Power is working in our lives. We marvel at the way things come together. Answers come in ways we would never have expected. Things come together in ways that surpass anything we might have thought of on our own. All we have to do – is the Right thing and we have nothing to fear. If we make a mistake, we just do the *next* Right thing.

Resolution

Now that God has my attention, I am grateful for my experiences and all that I have gone through. They have brought me close to my Higher Power. Today I actively seek ways to improve my conscious contact with Him. My relationship with my Higher Power is its own reward because when I have sense of His Presence, I am filled with Joy and my Faith is strong. It serves to strengthen my Trust. When I sense His Presence and have Joy I am filled with Love and I feel Secure. When I feel Secure, I have no room for fear and doubt.

Light

Thought

Goodness in our lives, in all its forms, is like Light from our Higher Power. Fear, doubt, insecurity and all their brethren are like Darkness. Darkness is not the opposite of Light, but the absence of it. When we shine a light into a dark room, the darkness no longer exists and the room is filled with light.

Darkness does not really exist. The room *appears* dark because there is no light. It is like this with all the negativity in our life. The negativity may be our depression, anxiety, fear, doubt, anger....you get the idea. But the negativity does not really exist because the moment we shine Light on it, it disappears. The Light may be in many forms; the touch of a friend, words from our sponsor, fellowship at a meeting, or a sense of God's Presence.

The negativity only exists because we nourish it. We feed it. One thought begets another and so forth. But the moment we allow Light in, it vanquishes.

It's our choice. We don't even really need to understand the fear, doubt, anger, or sadness. We don't really have to *figure it out.* We just need to know that it is not serving us.

We can *let it go.* We can *let it go* and allow ourselves to fill with Light.

Resolution

I can go for a walk. I can talk to a friend. I can read something inspirational. I can go to a meeting. I can eat a peanut. I know that when I experience negativity, it is because I am allowing it to exist. It no longer exists the moment I bring Light to the subject. This is important for me to remember because I am not a victim of my moods and thinking. I can do something to feel my Higher Power's Presence within me and around me and I no longer fear because I am filled with Joy!

Paradox

Thought

Sometimes the principles of the program are like a Buddhist puzzle. We surrender to win. And then we have to give it away.....in order to keep it. Darkness is not the opposite of Light; it is the absence of it. Joy is not the result of a wonderful life, but the cause of it. A pain shared is divided and a happiness shared is multiplied.

Things are not what they seem. There is the other side of the coin. We learn to take a closer look at our lives and our script changes. We learn to make lemonade out of lemons as they say. Our greatest weakness becomes our greatest strength. Our capacity for pain is only exceeded by our capacity for joy.

We begin to find meaning and purpose in our lives. We don't take everything at face value. We learn to look for the good behind every seeming setback. Gratitude replaces our cynicism and resentments.

Resolution

Our recovery and program is like building a house and starting with the foundation. We can look around and see the ground before us. We add flooring and stairs and before we are through, we look out from our roof. We see the same ground before us but our perspective has changed. Now we see the sky and the treetops. We derive joy and security from our new   home.

Clarity

Thought

The 12 Steps are a process of growth and change. If we are thorough, several things occur. We become *cleaned out.* This alone is nothing short of a miraculous process. We have the opportunity to get rid of all the garbage we have been carrying around all of our lives. We can be rid of the baggage, the unfinished business, the old resentments and conflicts, the insecurities that plagued us, that which would hold us back and that which would bind us down.

Tall order? *We think not.* If we are painstaking at this process and do not leave a stone unturned, we will be blessed with ability to be *here and now* and to live in the moment. The process of working the steps also brings with it comfort, joy and security.

Comfort from taking on this journey with our brothers and sisters in the program: Joy from uncovering the presence of our Higher Power: Security from the gained sense that you are being provided for and have everything you need.

Resolution

We can now move through our day in a calm and relaxed way. We walk with assurance because we always have the fellowship and our Higher Power as close to us as our breath. This is Clarity.

Dual Diagnosis

Thought.

We are dually diagnosed. We are addicts/alcoholics and have other mental health matters. Our drug use and emotional problems impact on each other. One exacerbates the other and vice versa. This creates double obstacles and life hasn't been so terrific.

Things…that you do not think are possible…are possible! Oh sure. Well, we often see it other people's lives before we seen it in our own and we must believe recovery is *possible* – first, before we can endeavor on the journey ourselves. Sometimes, in spite of ourselves, we have hope. It's as though we have some innate instinct of hope by virtue of being alive.

Pauline was a short, elderly lady that I stumbled across in the hospital….literally. (I was detoxing). I had wandered into her room by chance, probably drawn by her warm, alert, and knowing smile. By an act of Divine Intervention, Pauline was a recovering alcoholic of 25 years in for surgery of some sort. To make a long story short, she gave me her *24 Hour* book. And on the inside cover, she wrote, "dear scott, where there's a breath….there is hope……love, Pauline"

For whatever reason, I held to that like it was a message from God. (You think?) For years, I remembered those words. I kept coming back to them at times when it seemed that hope was all I had…if that much…and there were very dark periods.

Resolution

I can have hope today. That much I can muster. For some reason, I continue…even through the darker periods. Hope is a *door*. It comes after *need.* We experience need when we are *broken.* We can pass through the door with Unseen influences and people like Pauline. And then we can think about how she knew about hope…and how did she learn to smile like that?

Faith and Trust

Thought

Our Higher Power exists. Our Higher Power is good. Our Higher Power is in charge. We need not fear. Faith and trust are very powerful and there are distinctions between the two.

Faith is the belief that regardless of our circumstances, all will be well. Trust provides an optimism and confidence that goes beyond reason.

Trust involves believing things will be good because I believe they are good. This does not mean that we can maneuver the universe. It means that we are in touch with the truth of our underlying reality.

There *is* a law of attraction. How is that the addict out of town has no problem finding what he's looking for? How is it that the person in Recovery, runs into other people in Recovery?

Trusting in the Good means being raised Above affliction that may occur. Do you remember or have you ever seen a television antenna? When the screen was snowy, flipping, and crooked and the sound was distorted, you could adjust the antenna and picture and sound would become crystal clear and sharp.

Faith is believing in the good; that a bad situation *leads to* the good – the means justifies the end. Trust is *knowing* that the seeming bad *is* good and is an end unto itself.

Resolution

I exercise faith and trust today. I am beginning to see the underlying good in all of my experiences. I may not know *why* everything occurs, but I *know* that God *is* there, that he is good, and that he is in charge. I need not worry. I do what is in *my* power and then I let I can let go. I understand that faith is believing that resolutions are possible. Trust is acting like you have already received them.

Higher Power

Thought

You do not have to believe in God to have a Higher Power or to be spiritual. Most people can relate to the idea of having a *little self* and a *higher self* **within themselves.**

It is no stretch of the imagination to know that we all have base drives and *lower* thoughts, desires and feelings as opposed to those which derive from a *higher* place within us. When we are angry, depressed, selfish, resentful and the like, these are emotions driven by our *lower* self. When we act in a kind, generous, and joyful way; when we take the 'high' road we allow our *higher* self to dictate our behavior.

We do not have to act on our initial feelings. Just because we feel something, does not mean that we have to do it (like getting high or drinking). We can not control the thoughts that come into our minds, but we *can* choose what we harbor, dwell on, and do.

We can always seek the *right* thing to do by tapping into our higher self. It is always right there as close to us as our breath. We just have to listen. We must quiet our lower influences enough to hear what our higher self is telling us.

Resolution

I know that it is in my best interest to do the right thing. When I don't listen to my *higher* self and do what I know is best, it creates a problem for me and others. I may have emotional/mental health difficulties and I may have a substance use problem, but I know that I get a 'feeling' about whether what I'm about to do is good or not.

Medications

Thought

There are varying opinions about taking medications. Old timers in the program used to tell people they were 'still using' if they took medications. This is naïve or outdated thinking. If one had cancer or diabetes, one wouldn't think twice about taking medication. Some people have a misconception that because a problem is 'mental' or 'emotional' – it is not like a 'physical' illness. Nothing could be further from the truth. The field of psychology today is based on the fact that 'mental/emotional' difficulties are chemically related. There are thousands of research results to demonstrate this.

Some people decide (after years of substance abuse) that they don't want to be reliant on medication...like a crutch. I'm sorry. I have to smile when I hear this. Ok. It's admirable. But it is misplaced righteousness.

Medication can make a significant difference in how you feel. People who are legitimately dual diagnosed are more than likely, self-medicating when they use drugs. (What do I mean by legitimately? There is a difference between someone who just gets 'blue' versus someone who is clinically depressed.) If you've been self-medicating, you will better off using prescribed medication for several reasons. You will be taking something that is meant to target your symptoms. You will be taking a measured dosage of regulated content (in other words, you will be taking the same thing each time). You will be monitored and your medication managed by a physician. If it is not meeting your needs, it can be changed.

A few things to note. Most psychotropic medications need time to build up a level in your system. This may take 3-6 weeks. Sometimes meds need tweaking. One must be willing to go through this process.

Some people decide not to take medications because they don't like the way they make them feel. It is certainly one's right to do that. However, one may need to seriously weigh the pros and cons. And one may need assistance doing that.

Resolution

If there is evidence that I may benefit from medications, I will give it appropriate consideration. I know that taking medication is not a moral issue but a medical one. I know that getting started on medications is a process and I must be willing to do that. Medications are just like any other tool I have in my Recovery toolbox.

Why Me?

Thought

What **not** you? (smiles) When that was said to me, I said, "BECAUSE!" Why are we the way we are? Some people think they are cursed. Some say they were born this way. Others feel it is because of the way they grew up. For the purpose here, it doesn't matter why.

We are the way we are because *that's the way we're wired!*

Even if the way we are is the result of learned behavior, the result of our experiences, it becomes hardwired….as though it we were born that way.

Do you get this? It doesn't matter why because we need to accept it. If we are hating ourselves because we are how we are, that really doesn't serve us well. Acceptance is the key to serenity. This doesn't mean we don't tweak where applicable, but we stop beating ourselves for something…that *just is.*

Our mental health issues and our addictability really aren't our fault. We need not get involved with blame. However, when we do know our vulnerabilities, if there are things we need to change, it is our responsibility to do so.

Resolution

I understand today that I am the way I am because this is just the way that I am wired. The real issue is addressing my vulnerabilities so that I can be safe, take care of myself, grow in recovery, and experience the joy that can be mine.

Step 1

Thought

There are two main ideas in Step 1: powerlessness and unmanageability. The question one must ask themselves is, "Can I drink/drug *safely?* By safely, I mean without getting out of control and generating negative consequences. Are there legal, work, school, family, or psychological problems as a result of your using? Do you avoid social, family or other activities? Are often pre-occupied with getting drugs, using and drinking, and recovering from the effects of drugs/alcohol? Do you suffer from withdrawal effects? Have you developed a tolerance to your substances? In other words, does it take more than it used to in order to get the same effects?

Many people need to be broken before they become willing to recognize that they may use/drink against their will. Often people are relieved to know this is like a disease; not a moral issue. Any reservations or hesitation we have concerning whether or not we can control our usage, keep us from appreciating all the benefits of the program and may ultimately lead us into a relapse.

Sometimes we need to take o the 1st Step backwards. It may be necessary to take a look at how unmanageable our life is in order to see how out of control we are. Homelessness, financial straits, loss of home, family friends, jobs, legal and or medical problems, our own distress, dysfunction, and impairment describe our unmanageability.

Resolution

I know inside that I cannot control how I use drugs/alcohol but I can't imagine never using again. However, I can stay clean/sober *just for today.*

Step 1: Part 2

Thought

I'm also powerless over my mental/emotive conditions. I've never been able to have control over all my symptoms. They have made my life unmanageable: No question about it. Today I pray for the peace to accept what I can't change and to know what I can change.

I've learned that when I get high, it makes my symptoms worse. And then I just want to use more…as a result of my increased symptoms. My symptoms may include being depressed, anxious, and feeling down about myself. For some, thinking gets distorted to one degree or another. But in any case, drugs/alcohol make it worse. Using drugs/alcohol is something that I can change.

Resolution. I can uncomplicated my life significantly by staying clean and sober today. I can learn to manage my mental/emotive conditions. But that isn't possible if I continue to use. If I ever hope to minimize the affects of my symptoms in my life, I must stop using. Everything rests upon it.

Reservations

Thought

If we still have reservations, hesitations, or think we might be still might be to control our drinking /drugging, then we have work to do on our first step. Chances are, if you're reading this, you've earned the right. In other words, if you have found yourself in a meeting, if people are suggesting to you that you have a problem, or if you wonder whether or not alcohol/drugs are an issue for you....guess what? *It probably is!*

The way to answer the question is this. Listen to yourself. Really listen. Get quiet. What is the first impulse you have? If you have doubt about your ability to control your usage, chances are that deep down...*you know*...that you have a problem. What are you saying to yourself? When you listen without all the 'buts' and before your defensive responses kick in......what are you trying to tell yourself?

You know.....you *do* know the answer to the question if you listen to yourself. Not wanting to admit it....is more often the case.

Even those with years of sobriety may entertain the thought..."well, maybe *someday* I can use again" This is why we stay clean *just for today.*

On an unconscious level, we all want to use again. Despite all the negative consequences and all that we had gone through, there remains a *desire to use* underneath it all. This is what makes an addict an addict. We want to use despite all the reasons not to….on a completely irrational level.

We need to know that we are powerless over this desire. Only then are we ready to surrender. And then we are ready to be helped.

Resolution

Whether I am not yet clean or whether I have 20 years sobriety, I will take an honest look at my underlying desire to use. I am powerless to change that. So I *surrender:* I resign myself to this fact and I yield to recovery today.

Now What?

Thought

When we become aware that we are powerless over our desire to use and recognize how unmanageable our life can be as a result, we realize that we must change our way of thinking. We felt miserable with drugs and miserable without drugs. We were filled with fear and doubt. Yet, there is a newfound freedom in the first step. We do not have to use. We have hope that we, too, can find meaning and purpose in life.

Nonetheless, Step 1 creates a void in our life. We are no longer using and we ask ourself, "ok, now what?" We have hope but we need something to believe in that can alleviate the inner pain, suffering, helplessness, uselessness, guilt, and shame. Reality hits us over the head in our early recovery. We have a desperate need for faith and a salvaging need for sanity.

The pain drives us to look to a Power greater than our self , our desire to use, our pain and that could provide a means of living that offered relief and peace…and never mind anything beyond that like joy and fulfillment. Some of need to first allow for the possibility of a Higher Power. We turn to the fellowship, our group and the program to pave the way. At first, we see evidence that a Higher Power is working in the lives of people around us. Soon things begin to come together for us as well and we are grateful.

The hope that our first step left us with slowly begins to turn into faith as we become comfortable with our notion of a Higher Power that is loving and caring. We begin to use It as a Source of strength. We start to develop trust that our Higher Power can fill our fears with love and our doubts with assurance and we see that order is being restored in our life. This is Step 2

Resolution

As a result, we feel ready to move into action. . We had previously given our life and will over to the destructive forces of our addiction. Out of desperation we looked for another way. All we need do is allow for a power greater than ourselves in our lives. We *let it* in. We develop our own understanding about our Higher Power that is loving and caring. Faith emerges from our hope for a better life. Many discover that religion has nothing to do with it; anyone can have It.

Step 3

Thought

We are ready now to turn our life and will over to the care of God as we understand Him. We had turned our life and will over to our addiction. It didn't work. In fact, it was a tragic disaster. We finally realized we were completely powerless over our desire to use and had continued to use despite all consequences. Acceptance of our addiction was liberating. It gave us hope. We learned that a Power greater than ourselves could restore order in our lives and had a soothing effect on the state of our affairs.

On this basis, we took action, and *made a decision* to align ourselves with God. We were willing to place our life and our will in His Care. This simply meant to do the Right thing. And if faltered, to then just do the *next* Right thing. As long as we do what we know we are supposed to be doing, we have nothing to fear and can rest in the comfort of His providence and assurance. So we sought Guidance and Direction and took relief in *letting go and letting God.*

This is usually a gradual process. (I love the old AA adage, "How do you get to Carnigie Hall?...*practice, practice ,practice!"*)

Our Higher Power wants to be in our life, and involved in all our affairs – large and small. Later, in step 11, we seek conscious contact with Him throughout the day. No decision is too small to include our Higher Power and to begin to develop a relationship with Him.

We begin to notice a change in our lives for the better. Unwittingly, we take refuge with our Higher Power. Our hopelessness dissipates. Our fears, doubts, and insecurities begin to fade.

Resolution

We can't get enough of it. We immerse ourselves further into recovery. We seek it and cling to it. Our needs are beginning to be met. We are finding our Way. I was recently at an open meeting where a girl brought her mother with her. The mother shared as well and said, "I'm so happy….because my daughter has found her *tribe!*"

And so it is…we are a tribe with common culture and ties. It is such an elation when we bump into each other out in the community. There is joy and excitement in being with our brothers and sisters who *understand* us because they are *like* us.

Step 4

Thought

This is getting exciting but when you go to do your fourth step, you don't know what wonders lie ahead. It may help, before you get overwhelmed with where to start, that you are being led into what is quite possibly, the most liberating experience of your life.

The biggest reason people relapse is because of the clutter in their minds. Whether due to old resentments, unfinished business, unresolved conflicts, secrets, guilt, shame, fears, doubts, and insecurities from childhood, hurtful experiences, poor self-image and esteem, and pervasive discomfort with ourselves, our chances for long term sobriety are immensely improved if we get ourselves cleaned out. Recovery means change. The Steps are a process of change. Getting cleaned out is an integral part of change.

People often procrastinate with Step 4 because they feel it is insurmountable and fear what they might uncover. But we have the love and care of our Higher Power now and we do not have to be afraid any longer.

I suggest starting with your good qualities; it's a good idea. Having trouble getting going with this part? Ask some friends about your good qualities. You may be pleasantly apprised. Most of us may not be as bad (or wonderful) as we think.

Usually, we write a 4th step. We tend to be more thorough and it is beneficial to be able to look at it on paper. No need to be frightened. This is going to be a very worthwhile experience. We wish to be done with the past and put it away….not led around by the nose by it. We seek to be rid of old behavior that does not serve us well.

Resolution

Upon writing a 4th Step, we will see what aspects of our character we like and what we need to work on. It becomes an immediate relief as we begin to write. We now have to a way to resolve our shame and guilt. Our 4th step does not have to be perfect. We can add to it later if we need to. We try to be as thorough as possible. The 4th Step can be as long or shot as need be. There are no rules. Some will write volumes and other will write in phrases or bullets. We simply do our best.

Step 4: Part 2

Thought

There is no right or wrong way to write a 4th Step. Some prefer to use one of the many guides that are out there. Be sure not to get bogged down with form or style. You just want to get this stuff out.

My suggestion is that you simply start with what is right in front of you. In other words, what things are on your mind and bother you the most? When we start in Recovery, there are things that we are most ashamed of and guilty about. This is a good place to begin. This will inevitably lead into a dozen more things. Continue to write as things come to you…until there is nothing left! This approach alleviates the angst we have trapped inside.

You will find that things have a way of falling into categories such as: anger, resentments, selfishness, fear, doubt, insecurity, and so forth. Certain characteristics will indubitably predominate. These will become more evident when you share a 5th Step with a trusted confidante and even later when you approach the 6th and 7th Step.

Resolution

Our 4th Step, when completed, should be readily followed by a 5th Step – for enduring effects and results. Our 4th Step is no small accomplishment. It took enormous effort. The work we had done so far, our hope, faith, and our desire for even increased spiritual growth have motivated us. We now have anticipation around sharing our 5th Step.

Step 5

Thought

Addicts/alcoholics are good at keeping secrets. After all our work in Step 4 and uncovering our often-clandestine lives, it would be tragic to just stick it in the closet. Our surreptitious behavior grows like mold in the dark. We must bring it to the light of day and it will dissipate.

We choose who we will share "the exact nature of our wrongs" carefully. It must be someone we trust (though some people choose an unknown AA member or clergy). Often it is our sponsor, another fellow in the program, or a counselor. We like it be someone in the program for they are more likely to understand. Usually, when we begin sharing, our listener will also disclose common experiences. We fear that it will not be possible to accept us after hearing about the things we had done. We fear that no one did things like we did. We quickly realize this is not the case. This is what makes the program work: Addicts understand each other.

The whole purpose of Step 5 is to admit our innate characteristics with ourselves, God, and another human being because the process is extraordinarily *liberating*. By writing our 4th Step, we begin to see the deeper nature of our addiction. Left alone and kept to ourselves, these things infect us and will most likely bring us back to our drug of choice. The process of admitting before God and a trusted individual brings us to integrity. We have shame and have isolated ourselves and we need to clean these things out of our system.

Resolution

It is important to reveal those innermost recesses and not leave a stone unturned. We may not remember everything, but we do our best. We risk momentary embarrassment in order to avoid continued guilt and shame in the future. We do our 5th step right away. We keep it simple. We are exact.

It is a *tremendous relief.* We unload our secrets and are *rid* of them. We undoubtedly experience feeling of a real spiritual nature. We are thankful. Our 4th and 5th step have revealed some undesired qualities and we move right into Step 6 to ensure lasting effects of our hard work.

Step 6

Thought

Our spiritual growth progresses and our work continues. Step 6 may be deceiving. Many of us are not really 'entirely ready' to have our defects removed. We have identified our defects from our 4th and 5th step. I never liked the word 'defect' because it makes us sound like a tire factory reject. What it means really, is those undesirable characteristics and qualities we have uncovered.

Step 6 is about becoming *willing* to be rid of them, deceitfully more difficult than it sounds. Often we *like* some of those seemingly undesirable traits. It makes us who we are and we find after a while, that we really may not be ready to give them up or change them.

Step 6 can take time. It is only when those traits no longer serve us; that is, when we are no longer getting needs met by them. It is when we find, for example, that it is more desirable to be charitable than holding onto our inner arrogant perspectives. It is when we find, for example, that it is more desirable to involve ourselves in enduring spiritual pursuits than continuing to nurture our material desires. Then we become willing.

Resolution

As I endeavor with Step 6, I shall do my best to be honest with myself and not delude myself regarding my motivations.

Sometimes we wish to look good and be able to say we have worked the steps. An enduring effort will mean recognizing when we are truly ready…to be willing, that is. We surely can not force it ; we learn that quickly enough but we do the best we can and shall return to the step, or any step for that matter, when the need arises as situations dictate.

Step 7

Thought

We have already decided that our Higher Power must be central in our lives. We have also reached a point where we see certain character qualities, whether arrogance, resentment, impatience, selfishness, doubt and so forth, continue to cause us pain in our lives. We wish to be free of these characteristics. The truth is, if we are doing a good job with the 3rd step, we should find that we are already putting the 7th step into action. In the 3rd Step, we turned our life and will over to His Care. Essentially, this has meant, always merely, *trying to do the Right thing. And the next Right next.* In terms of our behavior, this may mean not succumbing to our negative and destructive characteristics. We're doing ourselves a favor if we can be rid of this defect or that one.

Resolution. We recognize that our true freedom means aligning ourselves with God and can now move into Step 7 gracefully. We have become ready to be free of our character defects and now we humbly God to remove these shortcoming.

Step 8

Thought

Remember, the steps are a cleaning out process. We achieve a sense of humility in Steps 1-2, that is, we learn to see ourselves appropriately in relation to our Higher Power. In Steps 4 and 5, we start to clean house. We inventory our lives, learn our exact assets and deficiencies, become aware of our inner nature and then we share it all. Our emotional burdens are largely alleviated but we don't stop there. We identify our persistent characteristics that we wish to change. Our Higher Power assisted removing our obsession to use and we believe that He can remove other shortcomings as well.

In our continued effort to clean the slate, to let go of the past and to be free of the influences and effects of leaving our affairs unsettled, we approach Step 8. Once again, we need to have willingness before we seek eradication. So in Step 8 we simply make a list of those we'd harmed – as though there were no Step 9. Our life is changing and we are no longer willing to be dominated by guilt and remorse. We receive a new freedom when we no longer have to avoid things or people because of our past behavior.

Resolution

Thus we realize the need to face our past with our new sense of spiritual growth. We seek forgiveness but the real deciding factor is our ability not to repeat our mistakes. Making an amend means making a *change* within ourselves so that it doesn't happen again.

Step 9

Thought

We make amends to the best of our ability. It may not wise to attempt an amend if someone is still suffering at our expense. We do not seek to make an amend if it may cause further injury. We do not put others or ourselves in emotional or physical jeopardy.

We are making amends for ourselves; we wish to be relieved from our past. Willingness can suffice when making an amend is not possible.

We offer an amend at our first opportunity. We are prepared for whatever response we may get. Forgiveness may not be provided. We can only humbly ask for understanding and do our best to resolve old conflicts. Our amend may be met pleasantly and old wounds healed. Our biggest amend is often remained clean and sober and ceasing to cause havoc by our using behaviors. But we know that we go a step further today and try to carry a message of recovery.

Whatever the response to our amend, we approached it with courage, faith and honesty and it will be met with spiritual reward.

Resolution

If we are painstaking in our approach to the Steps thus far, we have not left a stone unturned. When we do so, we become free from binds to our past and experience a sense of peace and comfortableness within ourselves. We become very sensitized to anything that disturbs our serenity and have a strong desire to deal with it immediately. We are ready for Step 10.

Step 10

Thought

We are human and we're going to make mistake. Our defects of character don't go away that easily and sometimes we become aware that a desire to use is still right there under the surface despite all we know. All of this is normal and it would not be possible to do things our way for so long and *not* have them reoccur in our thinking. Our serenity comes from not the absence of these feelings but the ability to cope with them.

We now know *instinctively* and *immediately* when something does not feel quite right. The 10th Step is about staying on top of things and not giving anything a chance to fester. We think about the day, write about it, and talk about it. And we address anything that disturbs us. In this way, we continue to take personal inventory. If something is wrong, we acknowledge it right away and set it right to the best of our ability.

Resolution

Some people become aware that they do this on a continual moment-to-moment basis. This actually sets the pace for the 11th Step as we seek conscious contact with our Higher Power.

Step 11

Thought

At this stage in our Recovery, we have become conscious of receiving guidance and direction from our Higher Power. It comes through other people and our own increasing insights. We realized certain persons are brought into our life and come to see there are no coincidences. We know are Higher Power is working in our lives. We are assured that He is *good.* We see that everything happens for good, for our soul's growth, in our best interest…whether we always understand what that is or not. We learn to *trust* that everything that happens is therefore good and we learn to meet even seemingly despairing events in our lives with gratitude.

We come to know that God also gives us the *power* to carry out what we know is the Right thing. We now use prayer and meditation to increase our contact with Him and to be aware of it in a tangible way. In our prayers, we ask for what we need and in our meditations, we listen for what we need to know.

We have cleaned house: we are a clear channel now. We live in the present. We are free of ourselves and the past. We are *here and now.* We can be ourselves. These qualities make us receptive to hear and know His will for us.

It becomes easier to seek His will for us because we realize that if something isn't right, it will become a source of dissonance to be contended with. We also recognize that our motivation is often prompted by a misguided tendency and inclination. Having suffered such consequences over and over and having worked so hard in our program, it is easier, desired, and sought out – to know what is the Right thing to do.

Resolution

Our conscious contact with our Higher Power is an overwhelming joy and sought out with eagerness and anticipation. It provides refuge and fills us with a sense of confidence and peace like we have never known before. We have a sense of well-being. We trust that our Higher Power will support us through any situation and have faith in outcomes. We cease to worry about anything. We are having a Spiritual Awakening.

Step 12

Thought

We are convinced that including our Higher Power into our daily lives has been the key that brought recovery into our lives. We had really just wanted a way to stop using. We would have been happy to just stop hurting inside. We never anticipated the fulfillment we were to discover. Who knew?

We discover that it is a gift to help others in their efforts to stop using. When we welcome newcomers, provide our phone number, offer a ride to a meeting, go for coffee after the meeting, and share our experiences, strength and hope, we are *carrying the message* of recovery. This is one of our spiritual benefits. We actually become a channel for our Higher Power to reach others. Often lessons learned were bitter and shameful. We find they were not without purpose: they brought us close to our Higher Power, they are now dignified by our ability to help others and provide us with self-respect.

We like ourselves today. We have become comfortable in our own skin. No amount of drugs could ever provide us with that. We practice the principles of the program that we have learned, in all our affairs, in and out of the rooms of the program. Our Recovery is who we are now as a person. We practice the principles daily not only because they resuscitated us but because we want to *keep* our grace and joy.

Resolution

Our spiritual awakening is a new beginning. We may be a beacon in the rain for fellow addicts coming into the program. We have been gifted to now lead fulfilling lives.

Economic Insecurity

Thought

The 12 Promises as provided in AA's Big Book make mention of our fear of economic insecurity. Losing this fear is central to our complete sense of well-being. At some point in our recovery, we realize that our Higher Power provides us with whatever it is that we need. This does not mean that He authors an open checkbook, but it does mean that we are going to be fine.

We come to regard our relationship with our Higher Power and conscious contact with Him on a moment –to-moment basis as sacred and with relish. It is it's own reward. We may be surprised to find we value it above all else.

It provides endless joy in living, assured guidance and direction, the power to carry out whatever His Providence may indicate, the comfort that we are never alone, and knowledge of His Enduring Presence.

So…we really don't have to worry about anything….as long as we do what we're supposed to be doing. As a result, somewhere along the line, we may find we have no fear of economic insecurity.

Resolution

I realize today that I may not have everything I may want but I certainly have everything I need. A happy man is one who trusts in God. A rich man is one who is happy with what he has. No longer fearing economic insecurity relieves us of basic doubt as to our continued well-being. What a sense of security we are provided with! What a gift! We are very grateful.

Being Alone

Thought

Being alone takes on different qualities. Some of us like to be alone some of us don't. Sometimes being alone is desired and we appreciate our solitude. At other times when we are alone, we may feel lonely. Then there are times when we are choosing to isolate. We need to find a balance.

Some people thrive on being alone and prefer it. This is fine. But it is important to include people in our lives so that we can share our thinking. It's a type of reality test. A plan may make sense in our minds until we give it the light of day and discover it may be askew. By the same token, those people who are never alone, may benefit from learning to be ok – when they are alone. Often, people do not like to be alone with their thoughts and feelings. How come? What is it that is uncomfortable?

Resolution

The recovery process, in a very down to earth way, is about becoming comfortable with ourselves – with or without people.

When we were using, whether we were with people or not, there was a part of us that was alone in our desperation. Our Higher Power and the Fellowship comfort us today. We never have to be alone – like that – again.

Double Whammy

Thought

We have a double whammy. We have mental/emotional conditions that can propel us to get high. Then when we do, it screws us up more than we were to start with. And it is a vicious cycle that there was no getting away. We didn't function well without drugs, but we certainly didn't function well with them, either.

There *has* to be another way! Whether we follow a 12 Step program or not, there are solutions. But we need to be ready to make some changes. Connecting with a power greater than ourselves is essential. For some, that is a Transcendent being. For others, it is the Higher Self within them. And we must include sources outside of ourselves. We need the input of those smarter than us and it is a good idea to surround ourselves with people that can offer other alternatives, possibilities, and answers. The answers are always there but we must find them.

Sometimes God remains hidden to us till we look for Him. If we believe there is no help or answers possible, we will never find any help or answers. When we believe that we can find ways to improve our situation, we find them.

There are things we can not change. However, *acceptance* can provide a tremendous sense of peace. Sometimes this is the change that we need.

Resolution

Having a double whammy makes things more complicated: There are certain things I have to accept. I have learned that remaining open for change and answers change my whole perspective.

Less Than

Thought

At my Saturday morning home group years ago, the term "less than" emerged. We discussed it and were in consensus. In one way or another, we could all relate to feeling "less than". Less than means never feeling quite right; like there is always something wrong. It means never feeling 'good enough', never 'fitting in', feeling 'impotent', never 'being right', always 'being wrong', always having a level of anxiety, always having a pervading sense of doom and doubt, always being uncomfortable with myself and so forth.

Being 'less than' plagued us. It was the sustaining reason that we got high. Some called it 'a hole in the soul'. Nothing filled it. Ever. No one. No thing. No drug.

Resolution

It was only after investing heart and soul into my program and recovery – most importantly inclusive of serious spiritual pursuits – that we find Grace. Relief. Wholeness and Completeness.

It's there. It exists. You can find it. (smiles).

X Factor

Thought

There are 'Earth' people out there who are able to use substances without any negative consequences. We are not one of them. They don't get out of control. They don't have work, family, relationship, emotional, legal, medical, social issues as a result of using. They don't experience distress, dysfunction and impairment as a result of using. We DO.

Why? Why can't we use like they use? The answer is because we have a certain 'X' Factor. They don't have it. We regard it as a curse. We hate it. We don't understand it.

Then we surrender all our angst about it. We'd had it. Don't want any part of it. We become willing to go to any lengths to be rid of it.

Resolution

Sometimes quickly, sometimes slowly, our obsession to use is removed, the pain stops, our 'hole' becomes filled. Our 'X' factor becomes a blessing. If it were not for our 'X' factor, we would never have gotten to experience the fulfillment we know today. The pain we knew is only exceeded by our capacity for joy. Those without our depth of experiences are not capable of this level of sustenance in their lives. We are grateful.

Scott L. Gourson PhD

Our lives are more powerful. Who runs faster, one who is running to something good? Or one who is running away from something bad? Our drive has more force. Our 'X' factor, once a mark of despair and degradation is now the generating source of our everlasting solidarity and happiness!

Meetings

Thought

Meetings are a blessing; a real gift. Whatever we're going through, we are reminded that we are not alone. At the end of a meeting, we see that we were a little askew when we came into the meeting. Meetings may not have the answer for all our problems, but they will get us through all of them. The fellowship experienced at meetings is the magic of the program.

If we think we do not do well in groups, that we'd rather talk to people one-to-one, or that we do like to share in a group, we really need to do ourselves a favor and try. We went to all lengths to get high, why wouldn't we at least put in half the effort trying to feel better.

Meetings consist of people who think they are unique. We are typically surprised after a short time, how precious our meetings become to us. We hear other people tell our story. We are not quite prepared for that. It takes us back. But it is undeniable. AA/NA/etc people are a tribe. We are amazed that we feel we belong here.

Resolution

Sometimes people go to 3 or 4 meetings in one day. In the beginning, we are often trying to get past the obsession to use. At other times, we may be going through something exasperating and meetings keep us grounded. Sometimes meetings become a social outlet for people. This is OK! Sometimes meetings become a lifestyle for people. This is OK! Today I will allow meetings to become the center of my spiritual program!

Psychiatry

Thought

We have been to many therapists over the years. We may have been in and out of many hospitals and/or treatment facilities. We know what it's like to be out of control. It was awful and it was frightening. Sometimes we didn't know it till later. We did things we would not have normally done: sometimes it was due to our psychiatric condition and sometimes it was drug induced.

The fear of unraveling scarred our psyche. It underscored our being. We would never *really* feel deeply secure. How could we? We couldn't trust ourselves to keep us safe or sound – literally.

We began to lose faith in psychiatry and our doctors and began to wonder if they could really help us. There were periods when we really felt we were destined to be – unhappy, miserable, dark, and cynical.

Let me tell you, the bottom line is that the only thing that may be in our control is to – *not give up!* Our hope must reach beyond reason. We can get better. It may be an act of divine intervention, but it defies us to explain just quite how it happens. We meet a new doctor, we try a new medication, things that didn't work the first time clicked later, we find a home group that *feels like home*, we sense our spiritual spark, we find a *gift* in reading, a burden is lifted and we find that certain things we did not think were possible – became possible!

Resolution

I can't afford to give up. At times, hope may be all that I have. We are told in the rooms of AA not to leave *until the miracle happens.* We smirk at the cliché response but *we stay* ....because . Because there is nothing else we can do and we pray that these crazy people know what they're talking about!

Sex

Thought

Sex is another area where we were out of control and no one wants to talk about it! The subject is usually left in the background and does not get addressed. People tend to think it is in a different category.

Let me tell you, whether it is drugs, alcohol, food, gambling, shopping, whatever, including sex: it is the same Force of compulsive behavior. We are not alone either. If we get with the right sponsor, we learn that our tendencies, inclinations, and behavior is more common than we think. We are hugely relieved but still shrink at the thought of discussing it or hearing it discussed. We will feel better, though, if we find a way to talk about it - with the right person. It may be a counselor.

We really do reach a point in our recovery where we do not regret the past or hide from it. We reach a point in our recovery when we have made it part of our recovery that the subject may bring up some mild and fleeting embarrassment. We feel it, accept, and then we let it go. This is probably as good as it gets. But this is really – quite good – and once again we are amazed to discover that "this, too, has passed". Our shame dissipates. It is no longer a pervading sense of humiliation when we are faced with ourselves.

Resolution

We didn't think it possible but yet again we are delighted to realize that these forbidden, locked-away secrets we were condemned to take to our graves were not the mortal sins we thought them to be. We would never have thought it possible, but in our recovery today, within our spiritual awakening and growth, our perspective on our past behavior has changed.

We are not proud of what we did, but our obsessions have been lifted, we are 'in recovery' with this behavior as well, and it has *lost its' power over us.* We actually no longer really fear our secrets being exposed. First of all, we have made peace with it. Second of all, it cannot hurt us today. The blemish on our soul heals. We are free of it. We feel *thoroughly* cleansed today and we feel good about ourselves – deeply!

Who wakes us in the morning?

Thought

Who wakes us up in the morning? God does. Did you know that? He didn't have to! He woke us because He has *faith* in **us.** He knows that we can do what is before us. Isn't that remarkable? There is another hidden message here: that is, we don't get anymore than we can handle.

We won't break. Well, actually we could break, *but we will always have the resources to help ourselves.* This is a comfort. We remember that God is good. We continue to do everything in our power to help ourselves and continue to pray for *tangible* results.

Resolution

When I wake in the morning, my first thought will be to invite God into my heart and mind. His presence soothes my deepest concerns and I remain hopeful that this too shall pass.

The Circle

Thought

At the end of a meeting, people join hands and close the meeting in a usual manner. This may vary from region to region. Some people balk if the Lord's prayer is recited. One does not have to speak the words. However, it would be a shame if the meaning behind closing the meeting were missed.

The circle reminds us that we need never be alone again. Our addiction and mental illness brought us to depths of desperation. We are grateful that we have found a home with others like us who understand where our disease has taken us. Let's be careful not to let our objections of program protocol interfere with the comfort and joy within the rooms. Our meetings are like a rose; let's not get stuck on the thorns.

Resolution

The circle is very symbolic. At convention dinners, the meeting closes in the same manner and it is very powerful to be holding hands in a circle with 2500 other recovering addicts and alcoholics.

Ready?

Thought

One has to *be ready* for recovery. And it is hard to say just when that is because it will be different for everybody. Basically, when one has had enough and is sick and tired of the grief caused by their addiction, one may be ready to stop. People get needs met by using and when they *stop* getting those needs met they stop. When the pain of using is greater than the pain of not using, people stop.

Some people are able to *get it* in early intervention. Others still don't get it after jail, loss of family, job, home, and all their money. No matter how far down the ladder people go, there are always 'yets' and 'agains'. That is, there is tragedy waiting 'yet' to happen, or waiting to happen 'again'.

The true measure of whether an individual will achieve long-term sobriety is not their willingness, not their length of time in the program, not their painful history. What will make the difference is whether or not they are experiencing the *benefits* of recovery.

Short of this, addiction's *call* will undoubtedly pull one back in.

Resolution

Often sobriety provides *relief* and *peace* from the chaos of addiction. People are often grateful and hold onto their gratitude. But this too will not be sufficient. All successful means have one thing in common: that is *change*. Recovery must include a change of thinking and feeling and behavior. If not, they will lead right back into active addiction. Immersion in recovery – meetings, people, literature, and activities go a long way to safeguard us.

Change

Thought

There are five basic ways for recovery. They are 12 Step Programs, psychotherapy, spirituality/religion, medication, and a solutions-focused approach (or some combination thereof). 12 Step Programs are AA and other groups that spin-off of it such as NA and CA. They involve attend meetings, working the steps and following other suggestions as provided by the fellowship. Psychotherapy is for the purpose of resolving lifetime conflicts and/or getting through crisis. Spirituality and/or religion include the involvement of a power greater than ourselves. There are times when medication is called for. Solutions-focused approaches involve identifying triggers to use and addressing each with a coping strategy.

Whatever means an individual employs, they all have one thing in common. ***Change.*** To borrow an expression from AA, if nothing changes – nothing changes.

Resolution.

Of course, the needed changes won't occur unless there is *willingness.* Willingness can be achieved through *openness and honesty.* This is the **HOW** of recovery.

A Secret Place

Thought

We all have, whether we think of it in these terms or not, a secret place within ourselves. We go there when we are alone, perhaps when we're lying in bed, maybe when we're feeling particularly vulnerable, and sometimes when we are just tired, wrung out and can do no more. It is a place where we can shut out the world and be at peace with ourselves. It is a refuge and often our salvation. We go there for our preservation as well.

Well, there is more to this secret place than we think. We will come to find out that we are close to God here: He is *right there*. Sometimes we don't realize it until we further develop a spiritual connection. When we do, we will come to seek out this place with greater frequency. And relish in it.

Resolution

God is there. Everywhere. But we must *look for* Him to be aware of Him. We tend to see Him more clearly when we experience a divine intervention or a 'coincidence'. To our delight however, the more we look, the more we see Him. We learn faith and trust and knowledge of His Presence.

HALT

Thought

We all have things that trigger our psychological symptoms and our drug usage. There are external triggers and internal triggers. External triggers are things outside of us like other people or places associated with our usage. Internal triggers are responses, feelings, or thoughts inside of us that prompt us to use. Four of the most common internal triggers are being *hungry, angry, lonely, or tired.* The acronym H-A-L-T is used to remember them more easily.

Any of these can set us up to not be on top of our game. They weaken us. We are not at our best. Our thinking is likely to be askew.

If we get hungry, angry, lonely or tired, we need to remedy it as soon as possible. But we must first get good at recognizing it.

Resolution

Part of taking care of myself in recovery today is making sure I don't skip meals, deal promptly with my anger, avoid isolating, and getting our rest. If we are angry we may need to remove ourselves from the situation. We need to talk with another in the fellowship as soon as possible. If we are lonely, we may need to get to a meeting or be with other recovery people.

We talk about our condition in order to put it out there. We can better remedy it when we do so.

Church Basements

Thought

Church basements are under-rated. As a Jew, I have probably been in more church basements than any other one that I know.! 12 Step meeting always seem to be in church basements. When going to a new meeting, look for the AA bumper stickers on the cars in the parking lot. Right church: so far so good. Find the side door that leads to the basement and listen for the laughter. Ah good! Found it!

Church basements are freezing in the winter and a little too hot in the summer but the ambience is always warm and inviting. Some meetings have a door greeter. This is such a nice practice! You can always get a cup of coffee. It's hot and ready. Often a plate of someone's home baked cookies or brownies accompany the coffee. You can be assured that whatever your state of mind you have going into the meeting will be graced with humor, levity, consolation, and equilibrium. One always leaves in an elevated state.

Resolution

If the walls could talk! Miracle after miracle takes place in these rooms! People learn to their utmost humility that things they did not think were possible – were possible. Hearts are softened, healed, and made a venue for Fellowship. Lives are changed and become an instrument for carrying the message of

Recovery. People find sobriety, then Recovery, and then spiritual fulfillment.

Partners

Thought
It is Said we are created in His image. This means that we, too, have free will. We have the ability to be better or worse than our given capacity. In other words, depending on our choices and decisions, our life's disposition is in our hands.

Free will is a complex subject and many will argue against it. Certainly, we turn our will over to our addiction when we are caught up in the throes of it. But by the same token, we turn our will over to our Recovery as well.

Resolution
Our Higher Power will partner with us if we want. This too is our choice. If you think about it, this is a pretty good deal! As long as we Listen, we will most assuredly have on Edge on life. While we may experience misfortune, we will always have the means to rise above. By rising above, we maintain the ability to meet life with Joy. Joy because we are alive. Alive by virtue of a Life Force. A Life Force that is good and providential. A Life Force that we are partners with.

Fake it

Thought

'Fake it till you make it' is a favorite slogan in the program. Actually, we're good at faking it. Many of us led double lives. We were imposters. We pretended to be one thing and we were another.

But now we use thus slogan to better use. In early recovery, we may not possess all the skills, qualities, and abilities to survive long-term sobriety so we *assume the role.* We pretend we know what we're doing. We fake it. We act *as if* we felt the courage to get through the day.

We ask ourselves, "What would it feel like if the obsession to use was lifted...if I didn't feel gnawingly vulnerable...if I knew I would get through these crises before me? We use our imagination and muster up the wherewithal to move forward.

Resolution

We fake it. We fake it until our dread and angst subsides. We begin to see that we are *doing* better than we are *feeling!* We begin to see that our feelings do not have to determine our behavior. We begin to see that we have risen above our feelings. We begin to see that we really ARE *making* it and do not need to merely pretend that we are.

Sexual Secrets

Thoughts

You know, nearly ALL of us have sexual secrets. And they are severely shame producing. We can't believe we did what we did. Or we can't believe that we are still doing what we are doing! The shame and guilt are overwhelming. They pervade any sense of well-being that we might have. Maybe we can't stop. Maybe we're afraid we'll do it again. Maybe we're afraid we'll be found out. It's mortifying!

If it is current behavior and we are unable to stop ourselves, *we ask God to be with us anyway.* Listen to me, we've *got* to talk about this stuff. When we do, it provides a relief valve from the ensuing pressure. Find *someone* you can trust. This may be a sponsor, friend, clergy, counselor, or lawyer.

Events from the past need to be disclosed as well because keeping these things to ourselves can be the thing that makes us use again. These types of things have an insidious, consuming effect on how we feel about ourselves. Underneath, shame finds its way into all the corners and recesses of our soul.

Resolution

Ok. We are **not** doomed to be guilt-ridden to the grave. The shame **can** be subdued. This can truly be difficult to conceive of but recovery is *full* of things we don't think possible! Believe me.

If one is still engaged in disturbing behavior, see someone. Often our actions may be substance-induced or at least propelled by our substance usage. We are in a much better position to deal with it clean. If you are upset over past deeds, get with someone. As soon as possible. You will be tremendously relieved. And you just may find that you are not alone.

The shame and guilt gets relieved as we grow along spiritual lines. As time goes by, we are less impacted by our mistakes from the past. We no longer try to hide from them or shut the door on them.

Shame and Guilt

Thought

Shame and guilt are most debilitating qualities in recovery and run the risk of bringing us to relapse. Once we get on our feet after coming in the program, we will want to begin step work. When we first come in, we are not likely going to be brimming with trust; this is understandable. Even if we move through the steps, we are not ready to share certain things. It is an intimidating thought to think of revealing deep, dark secrets in a 5th step.

However, we cannot keep these things to ourselves. They continue to fester. They remain under the surface. They main even be locked away but they make for a depression on our soul and ultimately affect us on all levels. We will never be free unless and until we clean these up.

The good news is that... this is doable. It can be done! Shame and/or guilt are not indelible. We must share this stuff with a trusted confidante. Our secrets need to be treated with the light of day. We *can* move past them but they must first be brought out in the open between you, God, and another human being. If our actions are part of a greater pattern of behavior, we're going to need to modify our behavior. We may need professional help to do this. If our secrets are mistakes from the past and we have moved on, dealing with them as part of a spiritual program of recovery helps us to achieve closure.

Resolution

No longer will our secrets create a pervading sense of guilt and/or shame. Any remnants of these types of feelings are *fleeting* in nature. We feel them, accept them, and then *let them go.*

Shame and Guilt: Part 2

Thought

There is a difference between shame and guilt. Guilt is feeling bad about things we have done. Shame is feeling that *we* are bad because of things we have done. Our shame and guilt let us know something is wrong and motivate us for change. Other than this, there is no useful purpose for feeling shame and guilt.

We need to deal with these feelings in recovery as part of cleaning and clearing ourselves out. We plan our compunction. We set aside time to purposefully review our action, our feelings about it, what was wrong and why. We make a determination not to repeat our mistake.

Now we are *done* with it. God has forgiven us. We need to be able to forgive ourselves. Our job is to live life with joy. Continuing to beat ourselves up about things is counterproductive and is not God's will. If thoughts of retribution keep returning, we dismiss them until the designated time for penitence.

Resolution

It is the Will of our Higher Power to live in a happy, joyous, and free manner. This does not mean throwing caution to the wind. It means dealing with life responsibly. Our grief over our past behavior is *not* healthy outside of the above.

While we cannot control the thoughts that come into our minds, we can determine what we harbor and dwell on.

That Morning Feeling

Thought

When we wake up in the morning, we generally are *not* feeling raring to go! Right? In fact, most of the time we feel depressed and do not want to face the day or even get out of bed. We can't put 2+2 together let alone gear up for the day. Anything and everything that is wrong in our life bombards us all at once and we are at a complete loss to solve anything or put things into perspective.

Usually, once we do get moving, we are ok. But it's murder until we do. We forget though, every morning, that the fog does lift in a little while and that we will be fine. It snags us every time!

If we could just *remember* when we wake that our confusion and despair is just grogginess…and that it passes!

Resolution

From now on, starting tomorrow morning, I WILL REMEMBER that my inability to function *will pass shortly* and NOT to try and do anything until it does!

Cravings

Thought

Just because we *feel* like getting, *does NOT* mean that we **have to!** For many of us, this is a novel idea. I will tell you a secret about cravings to use that those in early recovery need to know... a craving *will pass* whether you use *or not!* It might reoccur, but it passes. It is so important to know this. If you just wait it out, it will pass. And then you won't have to go through all the guilt and upset of a relapse. Think of the bullshit you just saved yourself!

And you gain power! Once you experience an intense craving and having it subside sometime later is a revelation because you have learned and now know that you have the ability to override the desire to get high and make the *choice* not to get high.

Resolution

There are other ways to deal with the desire to use. 1) Think it through. Look at what you are going back to, look at what you are losing, and look at what you will have to go through! 2) Move a muscle: change a thought! Do just what that means. Get up and move around. Take a walk. Go somewhere. Do something. Anything! Change what you're thinking about. Pick up a book. Look at the newspaper. In a few minutes the desire will pass!

Miracles

Thought

"Don't quit until the *miracle* happens!" says the old timer to the newcomer. The old timer speaks with a knowing smile and the newcomer listens with a hopeful heart. He wonders exactly what could that mean and his fantastical mind speculates...what would it be like if... I didn't *want* to drink; I got a *good* job; I could fall in love; my anxiety would *go away*; I could stop being so depressed; I would stop getting in trouble; my family would *take me back*; I had peace in my life...and so forth.

Recovery programs arc spiritual programs and operate in *Different* realm. When we do the Right thing, and the *next* right thing, and we continue to do that, our lives begin to change. We can see it the people around us. Their lives are improving; they become happy; they wear smiles on their faces! We gradually begin to see it in our own lives. Our Higher Power is doing for us what we could not do for ourselves.

Resolution

I won't leave the program yet. I can see that other people believe these miracles can happen. They are either all nuts or maybe it is true! I will wait and see for myself.

Heart and Soul

Thought

Meetings are at the heart of 12 Step Programs and the fellowship is its soul. 12 Step Programs are our God given vehicle for Recovery. We come in the Program to get clean and really have no idea how much more we are to receive in the process. It's almost as though it were part of the Plan...hmmmm!

We are in pain and are suffering and we reach out to anything that provides a ray of hope to get out from under our disease. Even atheists and agnostics... *reach!* All extend an outstretched arm, towards what we are not sure. It begins with hope.

First, we find that we are not alone. And we see that there are those who have gone before us. There are *suggestions* about how to become clean and sober. We are told that if we follow these suggestions, we need not fear!

We are given tools to work with. There are steps to use, slogans to follow, phone numbers of people to call, meetings to attend, and heck, there are even dances!

Resolution

I am my biggest obstacle. I get in my own way. I find reasons why I can't go to meetings, the phone is too heavy to pick up, I'm not into this God thing, and what's with the hugs?

If I'm lucky, I get a shiver of cold fear...and wonder if maybe I really *can't* stop? I start to wonder if I'm one of those "constitutionally incapable" people they talk about. If I'm lucky, maybe I'll try anyway...despite myself!

Faith and Letting Go

Thought

One of the greatest gifts that we can receive in recovery is the ability to let go. We often, in addition to our obsessive drug/alcohol use, may be obsessive in our thinking processes and are unable to let things. Sometimes it really is the result of obsessive-compulsiveness and other times our emotions have been piqued and we are unable to let go of resentments, hurt feelings, something someone said to us, a seeming injustice and so forth.

Our recovery has been about change. And change usually involves cleaning ourselves out of unfinished business, unresolved conflicts, guilt and shame and whatever else that may prevent us from being free of the past and living in the present here and now. We achieve peace and maintaining our sense of peace becomes our priority.

Resolution.

Along the way, we have found that our confidence has increased due to our growing *faith* that *all is well.* Hand in hand with faith is our newfound ability to *let go.* We know that as long as we keep doing the next Right thing and follow what we believe is God's will for us, everything works out just fine. As a result when new situations arise, we decide how to handle it and then *let it go.* We have the faith now that when we include God in our thinking and our lives we *can* let it go.

Things don't plague us like that used to in the past. Today, we are so grateful for our *faith* and our ability to *let go!*

On the Beam!

Thought

One of my favorite expressions from the program is being *"on the beam!"*. What beam? God's beam! It is like being in the 'zone' if you are an athlete or artist. It is when you find a space carved out of the universe where you are connected to yourself and to God. All else falls by the wayside. In the beam is when you are in the 'Right' place to meet your purpose here on earth. You are at your best. It is as though; you can do no wrong as long as you are connected.

Sometimes, we seem to just find ourselves there and at other times it seems to be elusive and we just can't get it.

When we continue to work the program, in other words, when we continue to use and work the steps (stay clean, remain humble, put our life and will in His care, get ourselves cleaned out, maintain our serenity, use prayer and meditation, and carry the message), we enjoy a spiritual awakening and walk 'on the beam'.

Resolution

It doesn't occur to us in early recovery that we can be 'on the beam' on a regular basis; it is too elusive and our lives are in turmoil and our minds are cluttered and our feet are steeped in the quagmire! But it awaits us. If we are painstaking in our growth in recovery, with integrity and godliness, surely, we too, shall walk on the beam!

Humility

Thought

People often confuse having *humility* with being *humiliated*. To be humiliated means to feel ashamed and foolish by an injury to one's dignity and self-respect. To have *humility* means something quite different.

When we have humility we know our 'right size' in the universe. It does involve shame or injured dignity. Humility means we act with modesty and are free of an inflated sense of self-importance, grandeur or pretense. We show regard for propriety and godliness.

Often, in our active years, we have an inflated sense of ourselves. We felt entitled to gifts of life and resented it if we were denied. In recovery, we must *humbly:* ask for help, hope our obsession to use is lifted, seek to remove the wreckage from the past, and pray that our lives become graced with a newfound countenance.

Resolution

Of course, some come into the program humiliated. Reality comes flooding back to us when we first get clean. But we need not be *ashamed* for having found ourselves in these rooms of recovery. It is not our fault that we have a disease of addiction but it is now our responsibility to seek recovery. And we do so humbly.

Scott L. Gourson PhD

Co-occurring Disorder

Thought

A co-occurring disorder to substance abuse might be depressive or anxiety disorders, bipolar, schizophrenia, personality disorders and so forth. This is known as a dual diagnosis or co-morbidity. It exacerbates our substance abuse and vice versa.

Question: Does one's co-occurring disorder limit one's capacity for quality recovery? In other words, can the way a person is wired prohibit them from grasping and/or applying principles of recovery? Is a person more likely to relapse due to a co-occurring disorder?

Resolution

The answer is that it is relative. It will depend on the nature of the disorder. Regardless, I have experienced individuals with severe, prolonged, and chronic illnesses such as schizophrenia and bipolar disorders comprehend that they cannot use safely. And they don't use. I have seen these same individuals enjoy the Joy of life and God in long-term recovery. Mental illness does not mean one is incapable of understanding what recovery means. Mental illness does not mean the inability for long-term sobriety or serenity.

Let me explain further. Serenity does not mean the absence of conflict, dysphoria, or other impairment: it means one has the *ability to cope* with it.

It is possible!

Thought.

Those of us with dual diagnosis often use drugs/alcohol because we are getting needs met by them. Typically, we are self-medicating of co-occurring disorder. This is not license to use, but it does help to explain things.

We *must* stop using before anything is going to improve on a real level. If we continue to use, we will not achieve the quality if life that recovery has to offer. We are reluctant to stop using because we do not think that it is possible to be free of certain characteristics of our disorder(s). What we don't know *yet* is that recovery brings with the possibility of things we do not think are possible.

We probably never thought they were possible, because there were things we did not know. Sometimes answers come in ways we never would have thought of. At other times, a different obstacle may be removed and serves to solve another unrelated issue. Or our insight grows, and is curative unto itself. Sometimes a situation seems to be Divinely resolved for lack of better explanation. Time takes care of certain things and we get better at coping with others. Frankly, there are new medications coming out everyday and prescription designers are getting better at targeting specific undesired behaviors.

Resolution

Believe me. You just don't know! I would not delude you. There can be resolution to things you would not think possible! Furthermore, things often come together in ways that you never would have expected and change or improve more wonderfully than you could have ever imagined!

But we must be clean first and follow recovery suggestions.

How to Recover

Thought

Can I still be in recovery if I don't believe in God and don't go to 12 Step Programs? Maybe. There are five basic ways to be in recovery. They are 1) 12 Step Programs. 2) Psychotherapy. 3) Spirituality/Religion. 4) Medications. 5) Solutions-Focused treatment. Or some combination thereof.

12 Step Programs are Alcoholics Anonymous or other spin-off programs (Narcotics Anonymous, Cocaine Anonymous, and others). Psychotherapy can help resolve unfinished business and unresolved conflicts. Spirituality/Religion can elevate people and actually help them to rise above certain behavior and issues. One does not have to believe in God to be spiritual: there are many aspects of spirituality. Sometimes medications are needed and make a decided difference in one's ability to remain in sobriety and implement principles of recovery. Solutions-focused treatment is developing individualized strategies for sobriety and recovery. One learns to identify triggers to use and implement new skills and coping techniques to deal with them.

Resolution

Generally speaking, there are two requirements that run through each of these means. 1) Change. There must be changes in thinking, feeling and behavior. If nothing changes:

Nothing will change. 2) Recovery must involve a power greater than you are because your addiction/co-occurring disorder is bigger than you are and experience shows us we cannot do it on our own. A power greater than ourselves can take different forms.

Gratitude

Thought

One of the greatest powers we have is gratitude. Gratitude has the ability to melt our biggest conflicts and dilemmas. It's a perspective maker and we can develop it in recovery in short order. It works like this.

When we come into recovery and are faced with the wreckage of the past, we are grateful we have a future to make a difference. Before we lament all the different areas of our life that we have a problem with, we become grateful that we now have a program that will get us through all of them.

Recovery must be gone about with Joy and gratitude can provide us with the Joy to approach any task whatsoever. Despite the seeming insurmountable amount of healing we must undergo, we are able to temper our shame, guilt, fear, pain and work we must do with gratitude and joy.

Resolution

Furthermore, *we are not alone.* We cry and grimace at first, but learn to smile and even laugh at our disasters because we do it *together.* Our pain is dispelled and our joys doubled as we share them all.

Talk with God

Thought

The more we have a sense of God, as a Presence, the more we can have a sense of talking with God. Conscious contact. Step 11 talks about it and I think I glazed over the term for years. The meaning eluded me and I did not know what I did not know!

Some may read this about 'talking with God' and think I must be psychotic. Well, better lock me up!

When you have a sense of God's presence, you never feel alone again. Because you aren't. You are a part of the Whole. Some people grow up with this. Some people have an epiphany or revelation. For the rest of us, this is a gradual process. When we proceed along a spiritual path, we experience moments of Knowing God's existence, 'coincidences', or divine intervention. If we continue along these lines, or doubt dissipates little by little. Our connection with God increases in intensity and frequency.

Resolution

Our 'thinking' about God, 'believing' in God becomes 'knowing' God in the sense of 'feeling' His Presence. Occasionally or sporadically at first and then perhaps daily and even moment-to-moment, having a sense of His Presence becomes an innate experience. We relish this. We live with joy. We pause during the day and talk with Him. We have, too, a sense of being communicated with. It may be by means of someone we meet, by knowing what we need to say or do at critical moments, by suddenly having a new awareness and so forth, but we learn to become more cognizant of it when it occurs. I know, better lock me up!

Giving Back

Thought

What is it about 'giving back'? Everywhere, we hear about giving back. It makes no sense to us when we feel like we have nothing to give. We may be buried under the mire of confusion, guilt, anger we may due to the state our life is in. But, you know, it's amazing, the moment we have a real sense of hope or that we are a part of doing the Right thing – we are happy to share it!

Go figure! We have been selfish, greedy, and self-centered, yet when given an experience of fellowship and glimmer of recovery, we too are willing to pass it along. You can see it as one newcomer helps another and shares his newfound strength and hope.

When given a particle of recovery, we are grateful...so grateful! It is nourishment to us and it is sustaining like no drug or drink ever was. At times, we are overwhelmed with gratitude, particularly when we realize that God is doing for us what we could not do for ourselves.

Resolution

And so we become *compelled.* We become compelled to find a way to *give back* or somehow – *do something good* – as an expression of our gratitude.

Solutions

Thought

There is a whole branch of counseling called "solutions-focused therapy". This is a fancy name for finding answers for problems. Its' purpose is to provide a fix for areas of life that trigger symptoms of our mental health issues and/or the desire to use drugs/alcohol.

We are *not* victims of our thinking. Just because we think things does *not* mean we have to act on them. Solutions focusing is targeting what is needed to fix a situation and implementing it. It is *taking action.* We can brainstorm ourselves, with the help of a counselor, or by sharing with friends in the fellowship.

This is not rocket science but sometimes our illness or addiction may prevent us from easy answers. Remember, our Addiction is invested in our continuing to use drugs and will do whatever it can to sabotage our Recovery.

Resolution

I will seek out a counselor, my sponsor, or another program member to talk about areas of my life that elude solutions. I may need help to first identify what those arenas are!

Money

Thought

For many of us, money is a trigger for anxiety and sometimes to use drugs/drink. In early recovery, many people share that when they have a lot of money in their pocket (like after cashing their paycheck), their first impulse is to go buy drugs. There is a certain *point of no return* when the decision to use has *been made* and there is no reversing it: in other words, after a certain point, there is no room for discussion, further thought or debate – it is a done deal.

For some, it may begin way before the cash has a chance to fill their pocket. It may start days before with the *anticipation* of getting paid. Some people are aware of this sort of thing, and others seem to get cold-cocked after they go to the bank to cash their check. There needs to be an urgency to develop insight and to know these things and other triggers about ourselves.

Resolution

There are things we can do. Perhaps direct deposit is available through our employer. We may need to have a trusted friend or family with us when we get paid to hold our money. There are no fail-safes but we can make it difficult for ourselves to get our hands on the cash creating time to put other coping mechanisms into action if we start to think about getting cash and getting high. We are creating awareness when we do these things and we talk about them and share them with our recovery friends and they at least become a buffer for us.

Boredom

Thought

Sometimes having too much time on our hands is a trigger to use drugs/alcohol. It doesn't take long when we sit down after a day's work or after waking up on the weekend with no agenda that our thoughts turn to getting high.

For so long, we have been accustomed to getting high as a means of entertaining ourselves. It is what we do. We really may not have anything else that we like to do. Drugs/alcohol has become our main and perhaps *only* form of recreation.

Resolution

We need to sit down and brainstorm. We think of things we used to like to do before we used drugs and we think about things we have always wanted to do. We make a list. If we are at a loss, there are tons of ideas available online or in bookstores. Some things cost money: some do not. Some things we can do alone: some cannot. We must prepare for some things. We must work things into our agenda and *plan to do them*. When we have no plans, we leave ourselves open for circumstance i.e. like when an old friend calls with some *good stuff* or we run into friends who are *going to the bar*. It is harder to deal with situations like these when we have nothing in place on our schedule. What do I like to do? What can I get excited about doing this weekend? Sometimes we may be gifted with a passion…and find something we just love…and can spend hours on!

Money

Thought.
Many of us are plagued with the fear of economic insecurity. In other words, we worry about not having enough money.

Resolution.
We do the best we can. We will always have *what we need:* perhaps not *everything we want.* It helps when we have a strong faith in our spiritual beliefs. *Doubt is destructive.* We must think, act, believe, and breathe that we have what we need and will have what we need. It is a rich man who is happy with what he has. If having *what we need* does not satisfy us, we need to do some spiritual tweaking! Nearly all of us are not faced with hunger or need for clothing or shelter. Regardless of our situation, we must think, act, believe, and breathe that our prayers and needs will be met *tangibly.* We must never lose faith.

There are fundamentals of spiritual life that emerge over time and practice. Practice means exercising our belief in a power *greater than ourselves.* We first see that the program provides us with some basic skills for survival without the use of drugs. We then begin to see changes and improvements in the lives of people in the program around us. We start to have a sense of changes and improvements in our own lives. We put more energy into our program: it seems to be working! We may experience 'coincidences'. We may experience Divine intervention for lack of a better way to explain things. More is revealed! We experience things that we never thought were possible! Our recovery exceeds are imagination! And at some point, we realize we have lost the fear of economic insecurity!

Internal Triggers

Thought

Internal triggers generally mean our emotions that propel us to use drugs/alcohol. We must become aware of what they are. We don't just get high because we feel like it. There are *reasons* why we feel like it. Often we are responding to our emotional reaction over something. Perhaps we were disappointed over a situation; maybe something angered us; we might be celebrating; sometimes we feel vulnerable and cannot pinpoint why; other times we may be anxious or depressed about our lives. These are all examples of what may lie just under the surface that we may not always be aware of that is moving us toward using.

Resolution

First of all, we may need to learn how to increase our insight into ourselves. All of the examples above call for using different coping skills to avoid overwhelming desires to get high. You will need to find which ones work best for you. Many of us need to sit down and talk about things in our lives on a regular basis with a trusted friend. Some prefer a hard work out at the gym. You can write, go for a walk, groom dogs...whatever it takes for you to become centered once again.

Drama

Thought

After people put down the drugs/alcohol, a not-so-unusual complaint is that they miss the excitement...and that life is boring. People may have trouble filling the void. There are a couple of things going on here.

First, there is inevitably a lot of drama around the getting, using, and recovering from the effects of using substances. We seem to get involved in a lot of 'situations'. Right? We often have to come up with one story or another to cover our tracks. And we got very creative sometimes. Some of our scrapes were dangerous. We also may have made a number of trips to the hospital. There was never a dull moment. We may have stole, schemed, scammed and lived a deviant lifestyle. None of it was good: but it was exciting.

Secondly, substance users are very ritualistic. We enjoy the *process* of getting high. This may include making the phone call, connecting, planning, retrieving, and preparing for our substance use. Our adrenaline might start pumping the moment we left work, got our cash, made the phone call, or drove to pick up.

Resolution

So there is no doubt, excitement played a big part in it all. Short of taking up skydiving, there is not an easy answer.

However, what happens for many is that the excitement is replaced by the gratitude that one no longer must go through the emotional pain and grief that accompanied their substance usage. Furthermore, there is a sense of serenity that takes hold in recovery.

Relationships

Thought

One common cause of relapse is relationships. And there are some common themes running through this. 1) People feel vulnerable. 2) People believe it is better to be in a relationship than be alone. 3) People are lonely. 4) People are overwhelmed by the needs of recovery. 4) People have an underlying need to be taken care of.

There is a well-known 'suggestion' in the program that one *not* get involved in a relationship for 1 year. There is a good reason for it! It can become a huge trigger to use because people are focused on the relationship and not themselves. It is necessary to focus on ourselves in early recovery because we have work to do!

The problem is that the biggest reason people do get clean is the hope for a relationship. So it is difficult to swallow the need to stay out of one for a year!

Resolution

Look, if you just can't peel yourself away from that someone, at least do not go into it blindly! The fact is these relationships rarely work. Many people wake up a year later and say to themselves, "oh my God, what did I do?!" Recovery must be the first priority. It *has to be!* If recovery is not always first in your life, there will not be anything else in your life for long. We must go through a cleaning out, clearing out process that recovery demands. It is hard to do this if we are starting a relationship.

Even down the road in our sobriety, relationships are a large cause for relapse because they impact on us so powerfully. Relationships are a challenge to those with strong recovery skills in the best of circumstances. It requires balance and maintenance of our recovery operatives – our meetings, tools, fellowship, steps and spirituality.

Lying

Thought

Some of us really became master storytellers! We led double lives! We had become imposters! It started small... a fib about where we went after work, or an omission about why we were late, or calling out sick because we couldn't get up and so forth. We got bolder. We became more elaborate. The biggest challenge became remembering what we said to whom!

Resolution

We are so relieved at not having to lie anymore! It is a huge weight off our shoulders! We didn't realize how much energy it took to maintain all those stories! We didn't realize how much stress it created! But now we are free of it! Free of it all!

Being Ready

Thought

There is something to be said for *being ready* for recovery and there are differing opinions about what it takes to be ready. Old school says one must reach their 'bottom' before they will be receptive for recovery. New school says prevention and intervention can be effective in bringing people into recovery. An indisputable fact is that it is a *process* by which people come to terms with their addiction and/or co-occurring disorder.

So what *does* it take? There are a few factors. We get needs met by our drug/alcohol use. If we stop getting those needs met or are able to find other fixes to our needs, we can stop using. When the pain of *using* becomes greater than the pain of *not using,* we will stop. When we are in recovery long enough to experience the *benefits* of recovery, we can stay stopped. These are all relative statements and the degree to which we satisfy these factors will determine the quality of sobriety.

Resolution. It will take what it takes to *be ready* and there is no substitute for this process. Unfortunately, the sooner we come up against the negative consequences our addiction, the sooner we are able to come to terms with it. This is just the way it works. If we don't have our back against the wall in some fashion, we will probably not have the motivation to change. We don't usually just wake up in the morning and decide to get clean today because it sounds like a good idea!

Addict Behavior

Thought

What is 'addict behavior'? What is a 'dry drunk'? They are basically the same: they are when we *act* like we did when we were still drugging/drinking even though we are now sober. It covers a wide range of behavior. It may be a pattern of lying and/or stealing. We may continue to be irresponsible about our commitments. We may be careless about our appearance or our housekeeping at home. We may continue to act impulsively without reasoning things out or act compulsively in other areas such as eating, sex, or shopping. Our work habits may decline or we may continue to lose interest in daily activities. We may begin to isolate again. Our other mental health issues certainly feed into this significantly as well

Resolution

Learning to recognize these areas may help us avoid relapse and at the very least, help us gain a greater understanding of our nature. There is a difference between being 'clean and sober' and being 'in recovery'. Being clean and sober just means we are not actively using drugs/alcohol. Being in recovery means that we are making the necessary changes to live in a Right way. A Right way means that we live in an accountable, responsible, and productive manner with integrity. We become accountable for our actions, responsible for our recovery and in our relationships, productive in a contributory way to the universe and we do so in a truly honest manner. Living in a Right way creates a clear conscience: when we do otherwise, it can create issues that begin to pile up on us and lead to relapse.

Being Truthful

Thought

When we were using drugs, it was difficult to maintain our daily obligations with our families, relationships, work school and so forth. As our addiction advanced, we spent more and more time getting, using, and recovering from the effects of using. We became very preoccupied and in an effort to avoid problems, we were frequently less than truthful. It became more and more difficult to manage our affairs smoothly. We said and did whatever was necessary to cover our tracks and get through the day.

Resolution

Once in recovery, it was difficult to abruptly change all of our behavior and the habit of lying often continues. We don't want to appear to be a bad person because of things we had done. We didn't want to hurt people's feelings. We didn't want to disappoint people. We didn't want to be embarrassed.

We may really struggle with being honest and truthful. When we are not, it makes all the other things we are doing in recovery seem to be a waste! But the fellowship shows us that we are not alone. Others have gone before us. We are understood and it really makes all the difference.

Push Ups

Thought

Guess what? While we're in here working on our recovery, going to our doctor, going to meetings, working the steps, doing service work and the like, our *Addiction* is out there doing push ups! Yep! It's out back there, working out and getting stronger. It's *progressive,* remember? And that doesn't mean just if you are actively using.

So what exactly does it mean? It means that if we relapse, in very short order, things become worse *than ever!* Many of us have gotten ambushed and cold-cocked by the disease more than once. In other words, it can appear to come out of nowhere and then hit us over the head with a baseball bat. Many of us for whatever reason may have talked ourselves into believing that *we really didn't have a problem* or that *it wasn't really that bad* or that *it was so long ago, I can handle it now* or *my problem was with alcohol, so I'm just going to smoke pot now* and the like. Some people report *just one day* having a drink or being with some old college friends and someone *had some pot and I felt like it.* Just like that, they *felt like it!*

Resolution

We can never afford to lose sight of the fact that our *Addiction* know just what it will take to make us use again. It knows just what conditions, circumstances, places, and people we need to get high. And it is always right there. We may have stopped its active progression, but we are never cured of its presence. It doesn't *go away!* When we are in recovery, we experience a *reprieve based on our spiritual condition.*

This is all to say that we must always forbear *vigilance.* We must always keep careful watch for possible danger or difficulties.

March 20 One Day At A Time

Thought

Recovery is *one day at a time* because to think in any other terms is way too overwhelming. It is really too mush to think we have to do *anything* for the rest of our lives. We can stay clean *for today* anyway: we'll worry about tomorrow – tomorrow.

Sometimes I think it is a mistake to honor 'clean time' because all any of us really have is *today.* Frankly, the more time we have, the further away we are from the memory of *what it was really like.* We stop remembering specific feelings and situations. We stop feeling the pervasive desperation. We know it was bad: it is imprinted on our soul. But our lives become removed from the wreckage.

However, we honor clean time, celebrate it, and give out tokens because it shows that the *program works!* Many newcomers tend to think people with a year or more clean are from Mars! (We are, of course.) But it just seems impossible to them; they think these other people were not *as bad* as they are.

When asked, "how did you do it?" The anniversary member says, "One day at a time!"

Resolution

Sometimes, one *day* at a time is too much. We take it *5 minutes* at a time. "I won't kill myself for the next 5 minutes". "I won't use for the next 5 minutes". Urges *pass* whether we indulge them *or not!* 5 minutes gives us time to *change* what we are doing, or *call* somebody, or *find* a meeting, or *pray,* or just to sit and wait for the 5 minutes to pass…and then do it again! And again. ***Until we are ok.***

Taking Care of Ourselves

Thought

Most of us were so preoccupied with our addiction that we didn't really pay attention to too much else. Our affairs became unmanageable and our health neglected. When we come into recovery, we must begin the process of putting our lives back in order.

We take stock of what needs to be done: debts organized, car repairs, housekeeping necessary, haircut, dentist visit, doctor visit and so forth. We take them by priority and slowly get our life in order.

Resolution

We start to feel good about ourselves with each undertaking. It feels good to be paying attention to all the areas of our lives we had neglected. Our sponsor or close friend/family member can assist us and prioritize things in the event it becomes overwhelming. We are beginning to deal with some of the wreckage from our past. For some of us, there was years of neglect and it does not all fall into place overnight. Little by little we start to get things in order. We find that we can get all the support we need in the rooms of the program. We are grateful and the job gets easier!

Yes, No, and Wow!

Thought

Often, we feel compelled to understand what is going on with us when we are uncomfortable for some reason. We may even feel that we cannot move forward until we do understand. Those of us who are really obsessed, stress over finding just the right words to express what we mean.

This is all fine if it serves us well. However, often people find themselves ruminating obsessively about issues, events, conversation and feelings or thoughts. There is something we need to understand about needing to understand: we don't have to. That's right, it's not necessary!

There are only 3 words in the English language that we need to understand. They are: *Yes, No, and Wow!*

Resolution

Either something feels good or it doesn't. Yes or No. Either we like it or we don't. Yes or No. Either it's something we want to do again or we don't. Yes or No. And sometimes it blows our mind! Wow!

In other words, keep it simple. It is not necessary to complicate things and often it is not in our interest.

Success

Thought

Success is a funny thing. Often, in early recovery, we are actually afraid of it! Yep. And it is often the cause of a relapse. We may be doing very nicely in our efforts to remain abstinent and reorganize our lives and then we relapse for seemingly no reason.

Sometimes we have this need to sabotage ourselves. Continuing to use drugs/alcohol and suffer its' consequences is undesirable *however* it is *comfortable* and *familiar.* Our newly achieved success is *uncomfortable* and *unfamiliar.* Success takes getting used to.

There's another reason why we sabotage ourselves. We don't *really* believe that it's possible. We don't *really* think that we can do it. We must move from a *failure* identity to a *success* identity.

Resolution

Just exactly how do you do that!? Well, being aware of it is the first thing. We may give ourselves negative messages all the time: calling ourselves names, anticipating failure, putting ourselves down, 'awfulizing', and so forth. We must begin to substitute positive messages for negative ones. Short meditational readings can help: so does prayer. Explore your strengths such as personal qualities, things you are proud of, and strengths others see in us. Use your imagination and *visualize* what success would be like. Set brief measureable goals. Celebrate when you reach the goal, like buying a snickers bar!

Doing vs. Feeling

Thought

Sometimes, even after being in the program for a while or even a long time, we still have feelings of not doing *good enough.* We may feel that there is always something *more* that we *should* be doing.

Some of this stems from our 'less than' syndrome: you know, never feeling that we are adequate. Some of it is from our guilt and shame over the wreckage we displayed for such a long time – like we have to make up for it or make up for lost time. In any case, we may feel *driven* to always be doing the optimum thing at a given moment. It may be hard to really relax.

Resolution

The truth is though, often; we are *doing* a lot better than we are *feeling.* And it is important to know this. After we have been in recovery a while, we may have done a decent job of putting our lives back in order: we are working our program, we have a job, family life is fine, and we are paying our bills and so forth. Yet we still have that nagging feeling that we should be doing *more,* that it is *not good enough.*

So we need to distinguish between doing a good job and yet feeling poorly. It's a job for *Superman!* Yes, that's right! Pray about it. Ask for help to see and know when you are doing well! (smiles).

The Glass is Too Big!

Thought

Are you an optimist or a pessimist? Is your glass half empty or is it half full? It is such an important question! The answer impacts on your life tremendously. We cast a spell over everything we do by what we feel about the outcome. Generally, things are just not possible if we don't first believe that it is possible. If we don't think we can...we won't. We may be self-defeating before we even start.

If you're not really sure how you view your world, keep a little log with you. Try to listen for subtle messages you send yourself and record them. Keep score. What's your first impression about this or that? Do you cringe ever so slightly or do you smile inside? Can you accept a compliment? Do you 'go get 'em' or do you 'go away'?

Resolution

If your responses fall predominantly into the deficit column, you can begin altering the score by consciously re-phrasing things. For example, if you were to say to yourself, "I can't do this (whatever it may be). It's too much". You might say, "I am adjusting to _____ (fill in the blank) and I am learning how to handle it." Do you see the difference 'spin' can make?

So, that half empty glass…is really *half full*…furthermore, the *glass* is TOO BIG! …because *all we need* would fill a glass *half the size!*

I use it...but I didn't create it!

Thought
When we experience success in our lives, it is a two-fold process. First, we have been given a certain Grace. It may be by way of a reprieve, good fortune, or an accomplishment. Our talents are God given and we may have been gifted with favorable conditions. It is important to recognize this. Gratitude is appropriate and synergistic.

It is also important to recognize that we are utilizing our gifts well. We are making good decisions and choices. We are doing a good job.

Resolution
It is the Right thing to give credit where it is due. In other words, we can feel good about our accomplishments and be aware of God's Hand as well.

Prayers*

Thought

Blesses are You, Lord our God, who releases the bound. Blessed are You, Lord our God, who has provided me with my every need. Blessed are you, Lord our God, who directs the steps of man. May it be Your will to protect me this day and everyday. They shall be satiated with the delight of Your House, and You will give them to drink from the river of Your bliss. May my prayer to You, Lord, be at a propitious time: Answer me with Your true deliverance. **Happy is the man who trusts in You.** You who knows secret thoughts. Blessed are you, Lord, who pardons abundantly. And it shall be that before they call, I will answer: while they are not yet speaking, I will hear. I have put my trust in You; may I not be put to shame.

Resolution

May the words of my mouth and the meditation of my heart be acceptable before you, Lord, my Strength and Redeemer. I have made you, and I will carry you; I will sustain you and deliver you.

God is right here with us but we may have to look in order to find Him.

Scott L. Gourson PhD

*Rabbi Mangel ,Nissan (ed.). (1992). *Siddur Tehillat Hashem.* Merkos Linyonei Chinuch, Inc. Brooklyn, NY

Staying Cleaned Out

Thought

When we come into recovery, we are so mucked in the mire of our unsettled affairs, unfinished business, unresolved issues, broken relationships, ourselves broken, and overwhelming emotional baggage that we don't know one end from the other or where to possibly begin. Little 83 year-old Alice with 25 years sobriety once told me there is *nothing* that can't be done *one thing at a time:* Even the seeming insurmountable. Through step work, meetings, therapy, medication if needed, spiritual development – we get cleaned out – without leaving a stone unturned. This is not just possible *but doable.*

Resolution

It occurs to us one day that we have done just that; we've gotten ourselves cleared out. We are living in the here and now moment and have begun self-actualizing to our fullest potential.

We can only do this through daily maintenance. We cannot tolerate anything that disturbs our serenity and handle it immediately through whatever means are called for. Usually talking it over with a trusted friend or professional is all that is needed. We *worked very hard* and learn not to let **anything** mess with it. It is precious. We have nothing else if we do not have our recovery for it will all go by the wayside.

Persistence

Thought

Persistence is half the battle. Actually, it is probably *more* than half the battle. That means that if you just stay with it...you have a very good chance of succeeding. Don't believe me? Try it!

If you don't give up, and don't accept not succeeding...*you will succeed!* When you were determined to find some dope, most of the time you did, right? It's the same thing, if you are determined to get your life turned around, manage your symptoms, and put the drugs down: *you will.* Remember my friend, little 83 year-old Alice, who says, "There is nothing that can't be done one thing at a time"!

Resolution

It should be a comfort to know that despite how insurmountable a task may seem that simply by being persistence can get you there! Once again, believing something is possible makes it so. And believing starts with hope. And you know what? Where there is a *breath,* there is hope!

Waking Up and Feeling Good

Thought

You know, everything else aside, this recovery business is just about being able to wake up in the morning and feeling good! It's really about becoming comfortable in our skin. Through recovery, that is our meetings, fellowship, medication if necessary, and working the steps, feeling comfortable with ourselves and feeling good in the morning can be achieved. Through the recovery process, we become able to deal with all of our pressing issues from the past and stressors of the present. When we do get cleaned out, our job is to maintain it. We know how precious our peace is and how hard it was to come by, so we respect it and treat ourselves with care.

Resolution

Furthermore, when we do get cleared out, we are suddenly able to develop ourselves and pursue our talents in a tangible way. We are, now, who we always wished to become *and it is a joy!*

Sanctify

Thought

Sometimes our 'friends' or our 'connections' almost mock us when we say are not going to get high anymore. It's as though they are saying, "yeah, sure, sure…" so very dubiously. And we may say it ourselves, we don't need any help when it comes to doubting ourselves. We are beaten down, often broken, and worn out physically. We know it *has to stop* because we simply *can't do this anymore,* but how? We are not even in a place where we can conceive of being *out from under.*

We must ignore the voice of impending doom. This is the first step in transcending the muck and mire. Freedom begins when you introduce a higher purpose into all the things that you do.

Resolution

We are ready to be Liberated. Our labor, toil and futile efforts at putting our lives together have given us a humble spirit. Humility prepares us to accept the Wisdom necessary for Recovery. You can choose to maintain this humble spirit through the realization of our cosmic proportion as human beings or carry on going in meaningless, struggle-full attempts and worldly tasks to bring you to your knees. *Your choice!*

Freedom

Thought

Why must we be broken in order to receive our Liberation? When a box is all sealed up, it can only contain the space within. When it is broken down, it is open to Infinite space. When we are all contained in our world, there is no room for us to grow. When we become fragmented, we need others. So much of us has been missing. This is when Miracles begin.

Resolution

This is now, not just what our life has become, it is who we are! It is not just an occurrence. We relish in our Freedom over and over again – every time we wrestle with the world or face inner struggles. Our Freedom is like a constant state of escape. This is why we celebrate our exodus at meetings on a regular basis. Our exile is indelibly on our soul and we never stop feeling our leaving it behind and our newfound Freedom. Should we lose that sensation, our recovery is in jeopardy. We go to meetings and live within the fellowship in order to bring our essential being out and to remember who we are.

Our Bond

Thought

Through the process of gaining our freedom, we have formed a bond with God. That bond provides us with the power to transcend our everyday world while working within that world and all of its issues. The bond is kept alive by continual replenishing our relationship with God. We perpetually transcend our addictive propensities and mental/emotional vulnerabilities. Our oppression, that is, our addiction and mental/emotional issues become the seed, which flowered our liberation. It burned in us until we needed to open the door for Air. In our freedom from our subjugation, we now move openly realizing our potentials.

Resolution

The gift of this transformation provides us with a new way of being. Having 'faith' pales in comparison. Our new Sense goes beyond thinking and believing. We have gotten somewhere our mind could not have brought us. Our soul has been Touched and we no longer have doubts or worries on any real level. Our fears die of neglect. We feel God's Bond and Presence throughout the day.

Miracles

Thought

They tell you when you walk in the rooms (of AA); don't leave until the miracle happens. Well, I guess there are actually a lot of miracles that happen but there are turning points in Recovery. One turning point can be having the obsession to use/drink lifted. Another turning point can be having stuck around long enough to be started to appreciate some of the benefits of Recovery. A turning point may be recognizing that a Higher Power is working in your life. For some, it's getting past those first 30 days, or 90 days, or 1-year markers. We have all kinds of revelations and epiphanies that can be life changing.

Resolution

Whatever it is that you need? Don't leave till it happens! Sometimes we don't get the answer we want, but the answer we get is bound to bring us to a better place. We trust. And we let go. The Miracle is often that things come about in ways we never would have expected and come together better that we could have orchestrated ourselves.

Getting What We Need

Thought

AA and other 12 Step Programs may not have the specific answer to all of our problems but it will always get us through all of our specific problems. It may not come with instructions for every issue we have but it comes with the support system that will help you work through it *each* and *every* time *without fail! You can count on it!* It doesn't get any better than that.

Resolution

Even if nothing were to be said, sitting with a group of recovering AA people is an experience of fellowship. It says we all share a common purpose, that is, an addiction and most likely another mental/emotional condition as well. Furthermore, we are committed to coming to terms with it and helping each other do the same. The NA fellowship states that the 'therapeutic value of one addict helping another is without parallel'. We must never lose sight of this. This is how we will get better. It is where we share our joys when we do. It is how we carry the message of recovery in order to keep what we have.

Taking On Recovery Alone

Thought

Some people don't want to go to meetings. There are a variety of reasons. People don't like groups; think AA is religious: think AA is like a cult; don't want to share in front of other people; think people are too focused on alcohol; think people sound like tape recorders repeating slogans; don't like the 'God' thing; can solve their own problems, think AA is stupid; are not going to say, " hi, I'm ____, and I'm an alcoholic."; don't want to go to a meeting alone; don't want to get called on; have to much anxiety about going; and so forth.

While there are various ways to achieve recovery, generally speaking, the nature of recovery for addiction and other mental health conditions include reaching outside of ourselves for a higher purpose. This is because we are our capacity for living is bound within the limits of our addiction and other mental health conditions and we need to move outside of those limits. Usually, this means being *pulled out* by some Higher Purpose. That Higher Purpose can be many things. It can be a cause, a goal, or a power but it must be something greater than we are. Generally speaking though, sharing with other people on some level is an essential ingredient. The nature of recovery from addiction and other mental/emotional conditions is that we are unable to do it alone. This is not because we are weak or not smart enough. Other people are one of the required forms of medicine.

Ego Tripping Inferiority Complexes

Thought

Along with our 'less than' personalities, we soon realized we were also on ego trips! What a bizarre combination! But we knew it to be true. For as insecure and doubting our place in the world as we were, in the next breathe, we knew that we were *special!* Right? For as self-defeating as we were, we were also very critical of everyone around us – at least in our minds. While our feelings were constantly getting hurt, we were cutting people to shreds.

The addict/alcoholic has a distinct personality. The AA Big Book refers to it as 'King Baby'. We might have been just a little bit difficult to get along with! No wonder we went through so many relationships!

Resolution

Much of our recovery is learning how to be 'emotionally sober', that is, learning to become emotionally *responsible.* This may mean acting, reacting, and responding the way we know should not according to the whims of how we feel. Just because we feel something does not mean we have to act on it. We learned early in recovery that just because we *felt* like getting high, did not mean that we *had* to get high. We felt accomplished and in control once we had experienced this.

Depression

Thought

Depression is not unusual for those of us with dual diagnosis. When we are clinically depressed, that is, to be distinguished from the 'blues', which we all get from time to time, we experience dysfunction, impairment, or distress as a result. If we are also drinking and using other drugs, obviously, we compound the issue.

It is very important we seek treatment for our depression. Depression more than other emotional conditions will keep us stuck in our tracks. This is because Recovery must be met with joy. Joy is a very powerful quality: it gives us the impetus to let go and move on, the lift to override our anxieties and deal with issues at hand, and the sense of well-being regardless of our circumstances. So it is very important that we clear the path of pathological obstacles such as depression, which might hold us back.

Resolution

Of course, we do this relative to our ability. We are all born with a certain nature and we are predisposed in one direction or another. But we do the best we can. The right medications can do wonders; the right doctor, the right group, and   often   most   important   is   the   *willingness.*

Our Pain

Thought

Why do we keep re-telling our story at meetings? And why do we listen to the stories of others? Why is our 'clean-date' noteworthy? Why do we honor the newcomer? Why do we listen so intently when the newcomer speaks? Why do we need it 'keep it *green*'?

Because our pain is the key to our resuscitation. It was our pain that drove us to find *another way*. Our pain was the springboard to our freedom. We take a Leap of Faith and jump far enough to escape life's gravitational pull. Now we look with a whole new perspective. We apply this principle to liberate all areas and elements of our life. In other words, we bring God into each decision we make.

Resolution

When we bring God into each moment of our day, we move with Supreme Confidence through our daily activities and we generate strong, joyful, and sincere energy that is bounced back to us with even greater force. Good things happen to us because we believe life is good. We need an open heart and mind to receive God's gifts. The Opening is made when we remember the pain and thank God for the miracle of Recovery.

Therapy

Thought

Counseling or therapy can go hand in hand with AA. Don't let some old timer in AA tell you that if you're taking medications that you are not clean. He doesn't know what he is talking about. The Big Book even tells us to see a doctor when we have medical problems and psychiatric problems are medical problems.

Counseling is skills oriented; that is, developing strategies and skills to cope with one's issues and crises. Psychotherapy is insight oriented; that is, developing understandings about ones unresolved conflicts and unfinished business. Both compliment the 12-Step process immensely.

Resolution

If you're lucky, you have a therapist who does not leave a stone unturned and when you are done, you're going to be pretty cleaned out. Again, if you do this in conjunction with 12-Step work, you're going to find yourself in a very nice place.

Sponsors

Thought

Sponsors are intended to be people that serve different purposes. Probably first and foremost is that they themselves be models for recovery. They need to be able to be available to us; in the beginning there may be more sobriety issues and later on more life issues. Our sponsors should be well versed in the 12-Steps and be our guide as we work our way through them.

Some people have more than one sponsor. This is ok but we may tend to manipulate situations by choosing which one to speak to about what because we anticipate a certain response.

In early recovery, it's very tough to come in to the program and be expected to select a sponsor but what you can do is to ask someone to be a temporary sponsor.

Resolution

Unfortunately once we pick a sponsor, we don't use them! A stigma can actually develop because we feel we *have to* call them. We were doing better before we asked them to be our sponsor! Well, that's ok! It is more important to use someone *like* a sponsor than to *call* them your sponsor! So if that is a problem, then don't formalize the relationship! If it works, don't fix it!

Waiting

Thought

Bring a good book! Most of life is spent waiting. Waiting for one thing or another...to be through with school, to get a job, to live on your own, to have a relationship, to have a car, to buy a house, to get married, to have children and so on and so forth, right?

Bring a good book! Really! We've got to enjoy ourselves *in the meantime* because most of life is *in the meantime.* The point is – Life. Life itself is worthy of it's own moment of Joy.

Resolution

We tend to be so oriented to think – *when* I have this and *after* I do that, *when* I.... THEN well, THEN – *there is another then!* But NOW...is always NOW!

It's a Process

Thought

Recovery is a process...as is addiction. What starts as having fun, experimenting, and socializing inevitably becomes a means of getting various other needs met. At the very least, it becomes our main way, perhaps only way, and certainly favorite way of coping. It may allow us to socialize with ease; it may facilitate sex; we can escape our troubles; we can drown out voices of doubt, reason, and fear; we can deal with our anger and so forth. There begin to be consequences for our behavior. At first perhaps, we are able to skirt the issue, but eventually we are forced to deal with our drinking/drugging. Typically, it may take several go arounds before people become convinced that they really cannot drink/ drug *safely,* that is, without creating more consequences in one area or another.

Resolution

We usually come into recovery and the program a little skeptical and unsure what to expect. We are fearful and untrusting but we are also vulnerable and desperate to find a way that will help us stay stopped. Sometimes we are overtaken by the spirit of the program, become filled with hope and the warmth of the fellowship and begin to thaw out. Still, some things are gradual: we usual gain a sense of a Higher Power working in the lives of our peers before we notice it in our own. The Steps are a lifelong process. Our obsession to use is often lifted. Our spiritual growth is relative to our receptiveness for things of this nature.

Hopefully, if we are diligent about our program, we will at one point, begin to feel comfortable in our own skin and can handle most things that come our way without too much anxiety. Most of us are pretty happy if we can do that.

It's a Relief

Thought

It's a relief when we can get through a craving without acting on it. It's a relief to discover that just because we *feel* like it, doesn't mean we *have* to. We start to feel some small degree of manageability. We start to take some relief in attending meeting and look forward to them. When a crisis arises, when there is a decision to be made, when we are upset about the day, we begin to see how meetings help and start to feel like the program may be working. It's a relief. And we start to feel grateful.

Resolution

So now we have a sense of relief and thanks. We don't know what we would have done if we had not found our way into these rooms because it is sinking in how desperate our situation was. It dawns on us that it became a life and death situation. We are relieved. Deeply.

Fly in the Ointment

Thought

As hard as we try, doing our best, for all our preparing, planning, organizing, no matter what we do it seems there is always a fly in the ointment. Murphy's Law? If something can go wrong, it will?

So despite all our efforts, there may always be something that isn't quite right. You can't help it. It seems there's always one more thing that needs taking care of. This can be particularly upsetting for those of us who obsessively, compulsively need things a 'certain way'!

Resolution

We just can't let it spoil everything all the time. Learn to expect it. Learn to accept. It's easier when we anticipate things being less than perfect and can save a lot of heartache. Just go...."oh, there it (imperfection) is again!"

Vexed

Thought

Some people are vexing...worrying, frustrating, and annoying! Whatever is going on, it seems whatever they have to say (or do) - is vexing. Some people are meddlesome and dramatic making issues out of everything. There is no pleasing these people and often the best response is *no* response.

Resolution

Learn to recognize when you are dealing with this type of person. It is best to just detach and not feed into their laments. In Recovery, we learn to take care of ourselves and the biggest message is to *be true to ourselves*. This means that our recovery comes first and should another be *vexing*...we can ignore them!

Co-dependency

Thought

Co-dependency refers to the unhealthy type of coping patterns a person develops when dealing with an active addict or alcoholic. It refers to the ways we try to take care of them, fix their problems, make all kinds of excuses for them, arrange their schedules and appointments, and rearrange *our* lives in order to take care of *their* lives.

We do this to the extent that our identity – is about who we are when we are trying to care for this person. Our mood is based on how well (or not) this person is doing. We feel *responsible* for their problems. Perhaps we feel we did something wrong that is the real cause behind their issues. In any case, we feel responsible to make sure they get the help they need…and if they don't, *it is somehow our fault* – as though it was *within our power* to make them better!

Resolution

We do not have that power. We can NOT make someone else better. They must do it. It is the **only** way. Just like we cannot do our children's school homework *for them;* we cannot do the addict/alcoholic's recovery *for them.* Our children must internalize their own learning process to do their homework. The addict/alcoholic must do the same. This primarily means *being allowed* to *be responsible* for themselves. And this means facing the consequences of their behavior and/or lack of responsibility. This is what causes someone to develop motivation for recovery.

Moment of Clarity

Thought

A moment of clarity in recovery is when, in an instance, we become aware of a vital truth that has eluded us in the past. It is most always quite useful to us in terms of our spiritual growth. We are granted an understanding that comes to us clear as day and we can't figure out why we never realized it before.

They may be moments of divine inspiration where we see a course of action, a plan, or an idea that will serve to have utmost importance.

Resolution

These are examples of what is meant in the program by *more will be revealed!* But they are more than that. We come to realize that these moments are direct communication with our Higher Power. This direct communication can come in many forms: moments of clarity, seeming coincidences, new opportunities that present themselves, instrumental people that seem to come into our lives at just the right time, closed doors, and new open doors. We learn not only to dismiss these communiqués lightly but to be delighted by them. We can only marvel at how these things occur and know without a doubt that they are divine providence just for us. Smile! Be grateful! Do something extra nice for the universe today!

The Nature of Addiction

Thought

There are two key factors to understand about our addiction. First, we are *not* addicted to any *one* thing. Addiction is about our *nature:* not the *object* of our nature. In other words, our addictive *nature*, means that we try to fill ourselves up on the with *inside* things form the *outside*. The *object* of our addictive nature may be a drug, a drink, food, gambling, shopping, sex, pornography, relationships and perhaps other things, which ultimately manifest themselves by impairment, dysfunction, and distress in our lives. **The objects of our addiction may be more than one and/or it may change. It is our *nature* that is the real issue.**

Resolution

The nature of our addiction seems to be a response to "a hole in our soul" that we are at a loss as to how to fill. It can take us a long time to realize that there is no filling that hole with substances because we *always* want more. It is a ***spiritual deficiency*** that must be filled with ***spiritual nourishment.*** We find that over time, working at our spiritual growth as outlined in the Steps, sharing our experiences, strengths, and hopes, continued sobriety, and incorporating a Higher Power/Purpose into our lives are some of the main ingredients that fill the hole from the inside.

Inspiration

Thought

Listen to those moments. We all have what must be divinely inspired ideas. Perhaps we are particularly good at working in a certain area and have experienced a flash of creativity. Sometimes it is regarding solving a problem, becoming aware of a calling, a novel idea, or an understanding; but it has a certain astounding and perhaps profound quality to it. We know it when we've had it.

Resolution

We can ask God to delight us. Sometimes we receive what appear to be 'meaningful coincidences'. Don't underestimate them. We get Help. God IS on our side and it's important to know that. When we believe and know that everything really is for our ultimate good, it opens the door to see the ultimate good. We may not immediately understand why things happen or how they could possibly be for good. If for no other reason than pragmatic purposes, it is important to believe that it *really is...all good.* It allows us to see the inherent good in life, to remain optimistic, and to appreciate those moments of inspiration,

Growth

Thought

At times, we become aware of our growth. We may now be aware of a new understanding that we have or how something that always used to throw us for a loop is no longer an issue. This new knowledge often provides us with greater impetus to move forward and tackle the next things that come before us. A mark of growth provides us with confidence and renewed belief in ourselves and our Higher Power.

Resolution

At such propitious times, we smile and tell ourselves that *next* time, we won't doubt ourselves and that our faith will be stronger. Gradually, over time and succession, our level of confidence does increase, our doubts wane, and our faith does grow stronger. We have a new, deeper sense of peace because we are learning that all *really is* well and *will be* well!

The Gift of Giving

Thought

Even the addict with no clean time yet has something very important to offer to the newcomer and the old-timer in the meeting. To the other newcomer, without knowing it, he can provide the comfort and support of *not being alone.* To the old-timer, he helps to remind him of the pain of active using and keeps the memory fresh. We all have something to give. It is a *gift* to give because it helps *us* to know we are helping another. Often when we are helping others, *we* are the ones who profit the most.

Resolution

When we are providing support to others, often we gain what we ourselves need because ideas begin to flow within ourselves. It is said that in order to keep the recovery we have, we must give it away. Sharing connects us with other people; it is the essence of the fellowship and the fellowship is the magic of the program. We all have something to offer whether we know it or not. Find it. Know it. Appreciate the joy.

Don't Do That!

Thought

Do you doubt yourself? Do you criticize yourself? Are you always putting yourself down? Are you constantly ruminating about past events? Do you think you will fail before you even start? Are guilt and shame the most pervasive feelings you have?

We must learn to think smart! We must ask ourselves, *does this serve me?* In other words, is what I'm doing productive? in my best interest? of use to me? benefitting me?

As we grow in recovery, our negativity has less of a hold on us. Our esteem improves, we begin to feel better, and we start to *like* ourselves.

Resolution

The program tells us to just – *do the Right thing* and to then do *the next Right thing.* So when we find and recognize that our thinking is **counterproductive**, we can practice changing our thinking. We say to ourselves, "Don't do that!" each time we catch ourselves engaging in thinking that is negative and counterproductive. We are invested in *doing the Right thing* and when we understand that changing our thinking is the Right thing to do, we give ourselves permission to do so! We then become relieved of these thinking habits we think we have no control over!

Scott L. Gourson PhD

Lift Up Your Feet!

Thought

"I will carry you..." These comforting are found in various prayers. When I was a little boy, we used to spend Sundays with Nana and Poppop. We usually went to visit Mamama in New Haven. When we did, we had to go over the bridge when crossing the river. Poppop would always say, "Lift your feet up so you don't get wet!" We would. Every week. And thought it was the most fun! Well, we lifted our feet and got 'carried' over the river every time.

Resolution

Whenever we have a river to cross, we can lift up our feet. There is a favorite expression in the rooms. It goes, " *I can't. He can. I think I'll let Him!* It's a simple thought: a lovely thought. Keep it with you!

Patience

Thought

Ugh! Patience can be so hard! We want things now. It's impossible waiting for things to materialize sometimes. But there is a process. Things happen in God's time. It's as though the stars need to get lined up and room made in the universe for our needs, hopes, goals, and dreams to come to fruition. There is no denying this process. There is no substitution for it. It takes what it takes.

Resolution

We must realize that things happen just the way they are supposed to. God is in charge, *not us!* We plan plans – not results. Results are up to Him. Everything happens for our ultimate good. Sometimes we get what we want. Sometimes there are things we need to learn. Sometimes the answer is no!...or not yet!. We maintain strong faith and we remain optimistic. Let us take peace in knowing things are just where they should be.

Nighttime Prayers

Thought

Before we go to bed to sleep is a very important moment in the day. This is because our last thought of the night contributes to our first thought in the morning. There are a few beneficial things we can do before going to bed. Some people like to read something meditative. There are many daily message books on the market. Find one that resonates with you. Nighttime is a good time to review the day – a daily inventory if you will. Why? Because you don't want to give bad seeds a chance to grow. Do you understand what I mean? If you did something wrong, were thinking irreverently, entertaining thoughts of using, said something inappropriate, and so forth, these things need to be kept in check. Some things will require action; some will require a change of thought. It is good to forgive those who may have wronged you, angered you, or vexed you. It is good to ask for forgiveness for your own transgressions.

Resolution

Whether we are pretty cleaned out inside or working on it, we don't want to create more negative karma. We don't want to allow more things to fester or snowball that are going to cause us more problems. This evening quiet time is a kind of checks and balances.

Morning Prayers

Thought

Our first thought of the day can set our pace for the day. There are many wonderful ways to start the day. Some may read from a message-of-the-day book. Some like to meditate or pray. Some ask for God's help to have a clean and sober day and free of pathological symptoms. I used to take steps 1,2,& 3 each morning: would remind myself of my powerlessness, that God can restore order in my life, and that I wish to put my life and will in His care.

Resolution

Find what works for you. Sometimes this comes about naturally. Sometimes you can give it thought as to what may be special and auspicious for you! Have fun with it. Make it an enjoyable process. You will look forward to it. Well, perhaps have a cup of coffee first! (smiles).

Growth

Thought

Recovery is a journey not a destination. It is fluid, in motion; there is no standing still. Either we are moving forward in our recovery or we are moving backwards towards our addiction. Whenever there is a decision to be made and one is doubt, ask yourself, "Is this going to move me forward in my recovery?" Should you hesitate or have a reservation or doubt, guess what? That should tell you something and we need to look at that concern.

Resolution

We are never done with recovery; it's not like a pie we take out of the oven when its' done baking. We are never – ***there***- and are done. Addiction lies within our nature and isn't going to go away. Generally speaking, we can change our behavior but not our nature.

Where am I in my journey today? Recovery requires that we have diligence. It needs to be in the forefront as we include something recovery oriented into our daily lives.

Trust and Respect

Thought

When we start to get clean, trust is always an issue in different ways. As addicts/alcoholics, we have to expect there to be trust issues from our family and friends. Our addict behavior has no doubt destroyed any trust level that may have been present before our addictions took off. We have to earn it back. We don't get to be upset about it with these folks in the meantime. We can share amongst ourselves the difficulty involved. We can all relate. The *only* way trust is recovered is through time and there is no substitute for it.

Resolution

Many of us have found that after a significant period of time in sobriety and recovery that gradually people come to trust us again, respect us, and in some cases, even look up to us the matriarchal/patriarchal figure in the family. We are pleasantly surprised to find that at some point we became the caretaker and no longer required taking care of ourselves!

Meetings

Thought

We continue to go to meetings even after years of recovery. The obsession to use/drink may have been lifted years ago and using/drinking may no longer seem an imminent threat but we continue to go to meetings anyway. Meetings serve many purposes. First of all, Recovery always needs to be in the forefront of our lives because the nature of addiction is that we actually forget the dangers, risks, and continued potential for harm if it is not in the forefront. And while our primary purpose seems not to be about a problem of using today, we go and talk about problems in life today. For many of us, AA meetings have become the center of our social lives as well.

Resolution

As we gain time in our recovery, many of us find that we really don't know a lot of people that drink/drug today because we don't really associate on a personal level with those who do. Our friends and associations are with clean/sober people doing clean/sober things in clean/sober places!

Anniversaries

Thought

Newcomers report feeling people with over a year in recovery must be from Mars. The thinking is either people with a year or more were not 'as bad' or the newcomer cannot conceive of the possibility of putting together that much clean. This is why we celebrate anniversaries publically: they show others that the program works.

Resolution

It is a one-day at a time program and none of us really has any more than today. This is because we can really only stay clean for today; thinking beyond that may be overwhelming. When life tests us, we can stay clean for today and will worry about tomorrow – tomorrow. Of course, tomorrow becomes *today*. In this manner, we can string a bunch of *todays* together. Anniversaries are testimony to the program and we all celebrate when someone has one.

There But for You Go I!

Thought

I cringe somewhat when I hear about an arrest on TV. There is a part of me that thinks what if that were me? I feel a little voyeuristic because I'm *very glad* it's not me! I tend to feel bad for the person, almost regardless for what they did, because I know what it's like to be in trouble. I know what it's like to be so caught up in my pathology, drug abuse or mental health that I've landed myself in a jam. I know very well that we are accountable, but often I identify with the perpetrator than the victim.

Resolution

Recovery is about making good choices. It's also about a certain divine inspiration, and no doubt, about a little divine intervention. I know I'm making good choices today but I don't take all the credit. Hardly! I've had much good fortune. Are you making good choices today? (Are you accountable for your behavior? It's not our fault that we have pathology, but it is our responsibility to do whatever it is to help ourselves…to be as healthy, responsible, and productive as we can!)

Collection Calls

Thought

I have an assistant make collection calls for me for monies owed to my service. I don't like to have to make them, but it is necessary for many reasons. First, I'm running a business, and can't survive on good will alone. Secondly, when we engage another's services for whatever reason, we have a *responsibility* to pay our bills. Particularly in Recovery, **responsibility** is a major issue. We often need to learn how to take responsibility for ourselves because no doubt, we abandoned many of our responsibilities with our pathology and drug use.

Resolution

Often we take on the task of assuming our responsibilities slowly. Sometimes they get in our face, like a collection call! But we must do our best to handle it properly. We can vent about it in our meetings or to our sponsor or to each other. But we must do our best to handle it properly. *Then, we can become **grateful** that we are now taking care of our responsibilities!*

It's a Process!

Thought

Our addictive lives did not develop overnight. Yes, we may have been born with certain tendencies, but our problems, crises, legal situations, relationship issues, money matters and so forth, did not happen all at once. It was a process. Our recovery is the same way. We grew into it. We were probably not ready to stop all at once. Chances are we hesitated, had doubts and reservations. Some of us think if we put down the alcohol, or the pills, or whatever... that is still ok to smoke pot, or just drink beer, or whatever. Our recovery is a process; it does not come to us all at once.

Resolution

Wherever we are at in our recovery efforts, it is important that we immerse ourselves, to the best of our ability, in recovery. This means being with people in recovery, doing recovery things, in recovery places. In this way, we are able to learn what we need to know.

If I Knew Then What I Know Now!

Thought

OMG: If I had any inkling what my recovery could and would mean for me and my life, believe me, I would have done it a whole lot sooner! Is there any way that I can impart this to you? It may not be possible, when we are in the throes of our active addiction, to truly conceive what recover might have to offer. This is because we are limited by the confines our addiction has on our minds.

Resolution

Believe that I believe. I could not do what I do were it not true. There is a *leap* in early recovery. We jump off a cliff. We pray, whether we know it or not, for a safe landing. We leap based on unfounded trust and faith that those who have gone before us in recovery are not completely out of their minds! Something tells us that Recovery may be possible. And we *have to try!* We may have no choice.

Success!

Thought

The truth is that most of us have a *failure identity*. Over the years, we have come to feel that we don't fit in, perhaps have not succeeded in one venture or another, have not had fulfilling relationships, or generally feel inadequate or uncomfortable in our own skin. As undesirable as any of these things are, they have become familiar and we have grown *comfortable* with them. Furthermore, presented with the prospect of success, we often *sabotage* the process.

Resolution

So are just doomed? Trapped? No. We are not. But change and success is a process. Remember, how do you get to Carnegie Hall? Practice! Practice! Practice! We must become open for change. We must allow that it is possible. We must be persistent. We must be honest. We must be willing.

The nature of Recovery from addiction and pathology is that we need others. The nature of Recovery from addiction and pathology is that we need a purpose *greater than ourselves.*

Our self-image begins to change. We gain some self-respect. We start to like ourselves. As our relationships and spirituality grows, so do we. We become freed up to become whom we always wanted to be. We find that we are able to be productive; we are able to accomplish. *We are on our Way!*

Celebrate Life Today!

Thought

What the heck, sometimes ya just got to put everything aside and celebrate living! Go buy your favorite cup of coffee, candy bar, ice cream cone, whatever is something of a treat for you and take time out today to just sit down and enjoy it! No spinning your wheels about issues of the day or worrying about this or that...breath, enjoy your few minutes, and have a little joy today!

Resolution

Sometimes we get so preoccupied with working on things and trying to fix our lives we forget to stop, breath, and enjoy fresh air. We can't focus on our problems all day...day in and day out...all the time. So go ahead and do something nice for yourself!

May 7 Secondary Gains

Thought

What is it that keeps you from getting what you need? I don't mean materially. What is it that prevents you from getting the help you need? Sometimes we are just very good at getting in our own way. We have reason after reason why we can't do what we need to. At some point, we have to wonder if we are not really just happy with things the way they are!

Resolution

Not peaceful and contented happy, but often, when we don't change things that we complain about, it is because we getting needs met by it! There may well be some secondary gains from keeping our life as it is. Maybe we get to feel sorry for our self. Perhaps we get other peoples' support, attention, and sympathy. Sometimes we're just *used to* things the way they are. Whatever the reason, we're stuck! And we may well be *keeping* our self stuck. Hmmmm.

The Past

Thought

Chances are, given the opportunity, there are things about are past that we would change. However, can we accept that everything happens for a reason? (Even if we don't know what it is yet!) Very often our greatest weaknesses become our greatest strengths. Furthermore, we may find that we no longer regret or have remorse over the past and no longer wish to shut the door on it!

Resolution

Our veteran AA members tell us that this is so! In the beginning, it is hard to believe this for sure. But we are heartened and encouraged by such a thought. Furthermore, the shame too, can die of neglect!

Complacency

Thought

Complacency means we lose sight of why we need to be in recovery. We can forget the reasons we are here. Yes, really. Addiction is a disease that tells us we don't have a problem. The farther we get away from our 'clean date' the more susceptible we can become to complacency. We can begin to think all kinds of things...."maybe I don't *really* have a problem...it was a *long* time ago...things are *different* now...perhaps it was *just* a difficult period in my life...I'm taking an anti-depressant now...as long as I don't do opiates again, I'm fine...so beer is ok, pot is ok...I just had a problem with opiates".

Resolution.

These are just some examples of dangerous thinking. If we find ourselves thinking in these directions, we *must* get with a trusted someone in the program and air our reservations. *These seeds can get planted when our back is turned.* The best of us have moments when our judgment is out the window but we cannot afford to let it fester and become septic.

A Continuum

Thought

We are either moving forwards towards our recovery or we are moving backwards towards our addiction. There is *no* standing still. Every decision we make may affect our recovery. When making a decision or when thinking about anything, we must ask ourselves, will this move me forward in my recovery or back toward my addiction? Should you hesitate in your response…that may tell you something! Our thinking and our decisions can be like a tug-of-way, especially in early recovery. We really *cannot* afford to let thoughts of using go unchecked. Because they plant seeds. And the seeds grow. So we must counter-balance such thinking with - thinking it through!

Resolution

When dealing with thoughts about using or if we are in situations where there is using going on or trying to make decisions about what to do, where to go, who to be with…it is important that we keep checks and balances in mind and not let slippery thinking get the better of us!

Economic Insecurity

Thought

Often, one of our last fears to dissipate in recovery is the fear of economic insecurity. Most of us worry about not having enough money! Many of us were significantly in debt when coming into sobriety. It may have taken quite some time to get out from under and get our affairs in order. Yet, we may continue to struggle to make ends meet at the end of the month. There never seems to be enough money. More money is better than less money, for sure, but what we are really looking for is *peace.*

Resolution

The key to losing the fear of economic insecurity is knowing that you will *always* be ok. Your Higher Power didn't bring you this far to let you fall on your face. You will *always* have what you need, because regardless of circumstances, you will *always* have G-d's guidance, direction, and power to carry it out! *That's* the peace! (Money is another matter. We may not always have everything we want.)

Getting to Meetings

Thought

In the beginning, people are often filled with reasons why they cannot go to meetings. Granted, if you don't know anyone there, it can be overwhelming. Maybe you could go with someone or meet someone there? We have to be careful we are not putting up obstacles for ourselves. That would be your addiction talking to you! Anything to keep you from getting what you need! You wouldn't have any trouble going when you were using if there was dope there! Right? We could go very out of our way and out of our comfort zone when we needed to get our drugs. It's just something to think about.

Resolution

Am I willing to go to any lengths for my recovery? If you are, then you will do whatever it takes because you know unless you have your sobriety, you won't have much else. If the answer is really no…why not? Are you still having reservations about being powerless over your addiction? Do you still think you can control your usage? Do you think it's ok to put other things or people before your recovery?

Isolating

Thought

Being alone is ok and there is certainly a difference be-tween being alone, being lonely, or isolating. Many of us appreciate our alone time, solitude and may even prefer it to the company of others. Sometimes being with others points out our deficits to ourselves. Nonetheless, it can be a healthy thing to be comfortable by oneself with one's feelings. It can work against us however, if it becomes isolating. Isolation *causes* a person to remain alone or apart from others. If we are just 'in our own head' without sharing or being in the company of others, our thinking can get distorted. Remember, *our* thinking promoted our addiction and other emotional health issues!

Resolution

So…we really need to strive for a balance of our time, which includes being and sharing with others. Later in recovery, people may find they are able to trust their judgment more and rely on their own counsel, but especially in early recovery it is important that we 'check' the clarity of our thinking by conferring with others. Our addictions would probably *like* to get us alone so it can start to go to work on us and bring us back to using: isolating us from our recovery fellowship may be the first step!

Holidays

Thought

Holidays, birthdays, anniversaries and other celebrative dates can be a trigger for us. They all can be typical occasions when we would have gotten high in the past. And they are particular times when others are partying. The same may be true for warmer whether when people like to be outside with summer activities and cookouts that often include alcohol and other drugs. We really need to plan ahead! It is important to have a plan for the day so that we are not subject to circumstance. If we have a sober plan, we will be less likely to respond to a spontaneous call inviting us to partake in 'festive' events.

Resolution

Too often, folks are caught seemingly off guard by holidays, other special days, or times of the year and relapse. Put it on your 'trigger list' and come up with a strategy to protect yourself. For example, there are often 'marathon' meetings on Thanksgiving, Christmas, and New Year's eve. There are often sober cookouts, pig roasts, picnics and other outdoor events sponsored by 12 Step groups in the area during the warmer whether. And there are usually conferences and conventions at other times of the year. Don't be caught unprepared! Our addictions *love* when that happens! It's a great set up!

Red Sneakers

Thought

Go buy a pair of *red shoes.* That's right! Go buy a pair of **red sneakers!** Why? (smiles) Because you just can't be depressed when you go around wearing red sneakers! They make you happy! Everybody smiles at you when you wear red sneakers. Everyone says, "Great sneaks!" or "Where'd ya get 'um?" I'm telling you, everyone loves red sneakers! It will change your day!

Resolution

I will learn to bring the kid out in me! I won't step cracks in the sidewalk today. I might get a tootsie pop. I might even watch a cartoon. I might, yes, why I just might go out and buy a pair of red sneakers!

Forgiveness

Thought

Every night, when you go to bed, make a conscious gesture to forgive anyone who has angered you today. At the same time, make a conscious gesture to acknowledge your own iniquity and ask forgiveness. Make a conscious effort to appreciate the grandeur of life and the universe and say thank you! Ask for a blessing. Your sleep will be sweet.

Resolution

At the end of the day, it is important to take stock. We immediately know what may have been troubling. It is not necessary to perseverate about it. Either it was good or it wasn't. We know if something is wrong.

Practicing the ***thought*** above corrects our path. We can wake up and move through our day with joy! When we practice this every night, we can stay abreast of our lives and not let things fester.

Refuge

Thought

We have within us a quiet, safe place. Have you been there? Nothing can harm you here; the world can be shut out. We get to pamper ourselves a bit in our safe, quiet place. It may even give you goose bumps! We may remember being here as a child, and perhaps have gone there throughout our lives. Perhaps we are not conscious of doing this; we may do it involuntarily. It is beneficial to be aware of this safe and quiet place.

Resolution

We can retreat here when we need to. But whether you realize it or not, you are not alone here in this safe and quiet place. God reveals His Presence to us here by providing refuge from our lives and the world around us.

What if?

Thought

What if you knew you were dying? Ok, I know, God forbid, that's terrible. Forgive me. But think about it for a minute. What things come to mind first? Are you afraid of dying? Afraid for loved ones? Feeling a sense of loss? Sadness? Are you upset because you didn't get to do this or that? It shows us what is most important to us real quick! The thought of dying in the near future has a way of cutting through everything and showing us what is truly important to us and many other things just seem to evaporate.

Resolution

What did you come up with? Are there things you need to do? Are there people you need to have a talk with? Are there differences that you need to put aside? Are there new priorities? Good for you! Now, go for it!

Possibly possible!

Thought

Remember when we said "things you don't think are possible, may be possible!" ? At the time, we were referring to your recovery. But it means more than that. It means that you might get that job; can finish school; can pay off your debts, can open that business, can improve this relationship, can make the move.....and so forth. What things do you put aside because underneath it all, you don't think it is possible.

Resolution

Well......can we change the language a little bit? What if, for a moment, we just allow for the *possibility* that *it IS* possible? We don't have to know how or even have a clue how it might happen but we are willing to allow for the possibility that it is **possible.** Ok. That's all! Now, have a nice day!!

Follow these steps!

Thought

Peace, comfort and feeling loved are within are reach at any given time. You can teach yourself to tap into it. First of all, know that God is with you. I don't care if you believe in Him or not. Pretend; just for the sake of this passage. Pretend because this is a *very* pragmatic and practical deal here. Second, God is good. If you can pretend He is there then this one should be easier! Next, assure yourself that everything that happens is for ultimate good. I didn't say 'how', I just said it was. No analyzing allowed.

Resolution

If you can do those three things, and if you let yourself ponder the implications of those three things, and if you allow yourself to generate strong feelings about them, I promise you that you are not going to worry about anything, you will know that your needs are provided for, you will know that you are not alone, you will feel safe and protected. Tall promises? "We think not" as it is stated in the Big Book.

Reading

Thought

If you love to read, it is a real gift. Reading is inexpensive, can be done anywhere and you can do it by yourself. Reading can occupy our minds in the most healthy way: it can relax us, excite us, interest us, help us wait, help us escape, and put us to sleep!

Resolution

We must find something that we love to do. It's a blessing when we do because if we love it, it can consume us, our time and our minds. We need this; it is so important to have something like reading. It can be anything that works for you: knitting, sports, playing guitar, journaling, drawing – you get the idea. If you don't already have something....try. Are there things you used to love to do but haven't for a long time? Are there things you've always wanted to try? Google 'things to do'! see what you come up with. Look for ideas and then go with it!

When the switch gets flipped......

Thought

Sometimes, through no fault of our own, our mental/emotional disorders kick in as though someone flipped a switch. How do you combat that? Our switch gets flipped and we go back out and drink or drug. Then the wires really disconnect. Right?

Resolution

There are things we can do to protect ourselves though. If we know that we have this kind of potential, we have a responsibility to keep certain supports in place such as our therapist, our medication prescriber, our case manager, our sponsor and so forth. We may not be able to control the onset of a psychiatric condition (i.e., a psychotic break or episode, depression, manic activity, audio or visual hallucinations, delusional thinking and so forth) but we do know when something is wrong, off, or not quite right. It is up to us to let our support people know and to get treated *before* it turns into 3 months later when we are really lost to the world!

Really Tough Situations

Thought

At some point we knew that we were addicted to alcohol or other drugs. We just knew….that we were out of control and were powerless to control our substance usage. There is a reckoning,realization, an inescapable awareness.

At some point we know that our mental and/or emotional issues and difficulties were not of the average variety. We were in a different category than most people. Our depression was not just feeling blue; our anxiety level was greater than what could be attributable to daily stress; our mood swings were not just ups and downs; our thinking was not just confused but disorganized and perhaps delusional; and our behavior maybe bizarre or frequently aberrant, and often inappropriate.

We have lost days, weekends, weeks, months, and years fettered away.

Resolution

We consider our options. Nothing has worked. We turn to a power greater than ourselves. We don't just decide to 'believe' in God, or start to go to church, or begin to pray everyday, but we give ourselves completely over with no reservations or holding back. We will now do whatever it takes and go to any lengths for sobriety, sound thinking, and acceptable behavior.

Progress

Thought

Happiness, joyfulness, and freedom on a regular basis is attainable through daily choices and actions. By choosing to do the Right thing consistently; by continuing to do the next Right thing should we err, things will inevitably improve and the quality of our life as well. We eventually see that a Higher Power is working in our lives and doing for us what we could not do for ourselves.

It becomes easier to accept the notion that pain we experience in our lives is for our ultimate good by learning to grow and make the right choices. We realize that all of our experiences are fodder for our soul's growth and we more readily digest 'bad' news in a different light.

Resolution

We look to see how this experience can benefit us and serve us in a positive way. We take what comes in stride. We're able to eliminate much of the drama. We stop vying for attention. In a quiet and unassuming way, we move forward and don a new perspective on our lives that serves to cut through to the chase and bring us close with our ultimate and true goals.

Let's Be Clear

Thought

It's not alcohol or pills or pot or dope that we are addicted to – well, we are of course, but it's not like that's the end of the story. The substance is actually just a symptom. Do you know that?

It's about our nature...the way we are wired. We have a sense of deficiency. Some of us are more aware of it than others. Furthermore, we tend to try to fill our insides with things from the outside. The things we use can change. It may be the drink or the drug, or it may be sex or gambling or shopping and so forth.

Resolution

This is not the whole picture but it is the basis of our addiction in most cases. It is important to know. It is why we can't use *any* substance safely, that is, without the risk of further consequences.

Mental Illness

Thought

We may well have mental conditions beyond our control. Depression, anxiety, severe mood swings, thought disorders including delusions and hallucinations. It has probably caused devastation in our lives. We have been powerless over it and it has made our life unmanageable.

Resolution

But it does not have to be that way forever because we can learn how to deal with it, live with it, maneuver it, handle it, cope with it! For real. Accepting it goes a long way. Listening to our support people and being willing to try, take, and stay on our medication is vital. We must learn about our symptoms and triggers and develop ways to function more effectively.

We can gain on it, even with setbacks, and include a strong sense of spirituality. Spirituality can make the difference between subsisting and living with joy in our lives. Please, know this is possible. These are not just inspirational words but based on truths witnessed and experienced!

When We Know It.......

Thought

When we know that a Higher Power is working in our lives we begin to gain momentum. Our faith develops and our trust increases. We were first aware and watched how a Higher Power was evident in other people's lives. Then we begin to experience it for ourself. With each seeming miracle and Intervention our sense of calm becomes more encompassing and thorough inside of us. Our belief in God turns into knowledge about God.

Resolution

We feel His Presence and anticipate it. We know that God is Present, ask for what we need, and marvel at the ways things start to fall in place for us and how our lives come together. We move forward confidently through our day and possess a sense of assurance that all is well and will be well.

Making It Real

Thought

We can accomplish more than we think we can. In the past we got in our own way and may have sabotaged our plans. Getting things done is usually 25% ability and 75% persistence. In other words, if we just don't give up and can hang in there – we will accomplish what we set out to do.

Resolution

Make a Plan. First, write down your goal. Now list what has to happen to accomplish that goal. Put them down by priority. Now write down the steps needed to achieve the first priority, Take out a calendar. Mark down tentative dates you hope to achieve this list.

Now, what can you do today that will bring you closer to your goal. Tomorrow? And so forth. Your 'to do' list will grow and change based on what you get done today. You are on you way! Now all you have to do..........is *to just keep going!*

Success

Thought

Let us not lose sight of our early teachings. If at the end of the day, we did not use, it has been a good and successful day...regardless of what else may have occurred. It's that important because we don't have a chance at anything else if we don't have our sobriety.

Resolution

As we move forward in our recovery, the obsession to use usually gets lifted and any strife we encounter is a result of living life on life's terms. We can get very involved and caught up in the dealings of the day and can easily lose sight of the basics.

Relapse

Thought

Sometimes relapse is part of the recovery process. It can have a jolting effect on us. We may realize – maybe we can't just stop. That's pretty scary. Maybe we are one of those 'constitutionally incapable' people we hear about in AA who can't get it. That's enough to make you get sober. Sometimes the relapse is bad. Real bad. And this time we KNOW we have to stop. Perhaps we were 'just' drinking or smoking pot but managed to go back to our drug of choice. We didn't expect that. We thought we could drink or smoke safely. Now we see we can't use *any* substance because it leaves the door open for further use. Maybe this relapse showed us we can't believe our own lies anymore.

Resolution

Relapse can have a purpose. However, if we keep relapsing we may be pushing our luck. 'Allowing' ourselves to continue to relapse is really making a decision to continue using because if we continue relapsing we never really stopped, did we?

Fellowship

Thought

When we are plugged in to the program, that is, we attend meetings, socialize with other recovering people, work a program, continually try to do the right thing and the next right thing, and provide support for other AA members, the love we get in return can knock us over. We may have never experienced the love, support, and care that these people provide for us. We are so pleasantly surprised! We may not be used to being cared for in this manner. We may not know how to respond. Our immediate reaction may be to recoil.

Resolution

But do not deny others of the ability to help, especially when you may need it. Remember, people *like* to help. Think how you feel when you are able to be of help to someone. Don't cut people off. Go ahead, feel the love!

Giving it Away

Thought

If we are lucky, we make it into recovery. If we work hard and keep true to G-d, true to ourselves, and otherwise stay the course, we will become strong and seasoned. Nothing can disturb you. Not really. Perhaps we momentarily become off balance, engage in the wrong decision or indulge ourselves but we've learned how to maintain and any lack of good judgment is brief.

Resolution

We feel assurance: assurance that all is well and will be well. We may reach a station in life where our greatest joy is giving away what we got. We feel we have been gifted. Not only have we emerged from darkness, but we have blessed with the ability to live joyfully, happily, and freely. And now we get to devote our lives to helping others do the same.

Master

Thought

We are all too familiar with our demons. Whether our demons are our obsessions and compulsions to get high, have sex, buy nice things, eat, be a victim of our own minds.........whether we succumb to depression, anxiety, delusion or hallucination........whether we are powerless over our moods and/or aberrant behavior – we know the insidiousness of our personal nemesis.

Our journey and our purpose is largely about mastering our nature. We are consumed by our struggle and our drive to come out on top. And *we can.*

Resolution

There may certainly be things that we cannot change. We learn to understand what we cannot change and what we can. We also to learn to accept and let go. We realize that God may do for us what we cannot do for ourselves. We may, to our delight, discover things we thought not possible were indeed possible! And we are left to marvel at how they came about.

Integrated Care

Thought

At some point we knew that we were addicted to alcohol or other drugs. We just knew….that we were out of control and were powerless to control our substance usage. There is a reckoning, a realization, an inescapable awareness.

At some point we know that our mental and/or emotional issues and difficulties were not of the average variety. We were in a different category than most people. Our depression was not just feeling blue; our anxiety level was greater than what could be attributable to daily stress; our mood swings were not just ups and downs; our thinking was not just confused but disorganized and perhaps delusional; and our behavior maybe bizarre or frequently aberrant, and often inappropriate.

We have lost days, weekends, weeks, months, and years fettered away.

We consider our options. Nothing has worked. We turn to a power greater than ourselves. We don't just decide to 'believe' in God, or start to go to church, or begin to pray everyday, but we give ourselves completely over with no reservations or holding back. We will now do whatever it takes and go to any lengths for sobriety, sound thinking, and acceptable behavior.

Resolution

Happiness, joyfulness, and freedom on a regular basis is attainable through daily choices and actions. By choosing to do the Right thing consistently; by continuing to do the next Right thing should we err, things will inevitably improve and the quality of our life as well. We eventually see that a Higher Power is working in our lives and doing for us what we could not do for ourselves.

It becomes easier to accept the notion that pain we experience in our lives is for our ultimate good by learning to grow and make the right choices. We realize that all of our experiences are fodder for our soul's growth and we more readily digest 'bad' news in a different light.

We look to see how this experience can benefit us and serve us in a positive way. We take what comes in stride. We're able to eliminate much of the drama. We stop vying for attention. In a quiet and unassuming way, we move forward and don a new perspective on our lives that serves to cut through to the chase and bring us close with our ultimate and true goals.

Refuge

Thought

There are times when we may be so worn down, beat, can't catch air that we just simply have no strength and are in a weakened condition. It is **NOT** an excuse to let yourself become depressed as susceptible as we may be, tempting as it may be and as vulnerable as we feel.

Resolution

What we can do is seek refuge, a safe harbor, protection from the storm while we rest and heal. Depression is counter productive. Refuge is nurturing and loving until we can one day resume our drive to change lives and save souls.

Priorities

Thought
When we have had a brush with death, our priorities can become very clear and simple. We quickly see what is important and what is not.

Resolution
Time spent worrying about what we don't have is time we could have spent appreciating all the things we do have!

Letting Ourselves Be Taken Care of

Thought

We are our own responsibility, of course, but there are times when we must rely on others to care for us or tell us what we need to hear. Most of us thrive on our autonomy and this is really tough to do. We may be care takers ourselves and are more comfortable and used to being on the giving side. It is important to recognize when we really do need help: it may be a difficult situation, emotional turmoil, physical illness and so forth.

Resolution

My father told me to surround myself with people smarter than I was. It's really very good advice; we can't be experts in all areas.....medicine, taxes, education, and working out are just some examples. It's a sign of strength when we are able to allow others to pave the way because there are circumstances when it may be the wise thing to do!

A Higher Purpose

Thought

There are certain, regardless of your orientation, that are essential for Recovery. One of the basics, most important qualities is possessing a Higher Purpose in life *other than yourself!* I didn't say higher *power,* right? But Higher *Purpose.* Some people are not able to bring a Transcendental (i.e. God) into their scope of reality. And that's fine, however, our addiction is way bigger than we are. (Do you doubt that? This is why we are unable to control it.)

Resolution

Our addiction IS bigger than we are and we need something **greater** to combat it. A Higher Purpose might be the welfare of our children, finishing college, becoming our own boss in a business and so forth. We need a purpose that we believe in so powerfully that it can lift us out if the mire of our addictions.

We Can't Do It Alone!

Thought

Another essential component to our Recovery is the understanding that we can not do this on our own. The *nature* of recovery from addiction is that we *need* other people to aid us. Sorry to all of us....*I'm going to do it myself* – ers! It just does not work that way! Why?

Because our thinking is limited by the perimeters and confines of our addicted minds and thinking! We need people outside of us to point out our hazardous thinking. When we are in early recovery, our *nature* is to use. We are still under the power of our addiction. And our addiction will call use back. It will create situations to make us *choose* to use again! Remember, we are either moving forward towards recovery or back towards active addiction.

Resolution

We can make decisions in early recovery that make perfect sense to us but upon closer inspection would really tend to lead us right back where we started. It takes someone with clarity in recovery to see and know that

The Barber Shop

Thought

If you hang around the barber shop, you're probably going to get a haircut! What the heck is that supposed to mean? Well, if we continue to go to bars and parties and hang out with people who use, chances are, at some point, we are going to use again ourselves. I don't care how many times you have done it and it didn't *bother* you and you have *tested* yourself, sooner or later you are apt to pick up again. Because it **sinks in** and **saturates** us! Gradually, we see it and want it. It lowers our resolve.

Resolution

People in recovery need to be with people in recovery and to be **immersed** in recovery..........and sobriety is hard enough at that! We don't need teasing, coaxing, enticing and seducing! Even just those beer commercials with all those beautiful people having so much fun sit on our addicted brains! Right? Don't you want to be out on that amazing schooner on that sun drenched day with the music and lovely smiles?

Where Am I?

Thought

Vigilence is another essential quality in recovery. We must *always* know where we are at and what we are doing to the best of our ability. We must *always* use the framework of recovery when reviewing our lives. In other words, we can never lose sight of the fact that we are addicts and are experiencing recovery due to a spiritual reprieve. Our recovery is based on our spiritual condition and we must guard against our tendencies towards addiction. We must watch our thinking and our behavior.

Resolution

Vigilence comes naturally after practice. We learn to look at things we do and decide in terms of the effect it can have on our recovery. Our new found serenity is *precious*.....we worked hard for it......and the second anything disturbs us we attend to it immediately. We learn to ask ourselves *everyday;* "Where am I ?"

Don't Stray

Thought

Some would like to think that once they stop using it's a done deal. Others don't like 12 step programs because recovery from alcoholism/addiction seems to be the driving force in everyone's lives and now that they have stopped using, they resent it being at the center of things all the time.

Mistake. Our recovery *from our addiction* must be in the forefront and if we think otherwise, we probably have reservations about really stopping or are minimizing the impact and power of our addiction.

Resolution

Recovery and maintaining sobriety is going to be hard enough *with* all the right recovery tools. Our addiction, remember, is motivated to keep us using, and it allows us to *forget* the depths we sank to and to delude ourselves that we will have it under control this time.

Saying Your Prayers!

Thought

First thing after you open your eyes in the morning, ask God to help you have a clean and sober day and do the first the steps in your head. Tell God you are powerless over your addiction and it makes your life unmanageable. Then let Him know that you believe that He can make your life sane (sound). Then tell Him that you wish to put your life and will in His care; that you want to do the Right thing and then the next Right thing.

At night before you go to bed, thank Him for your clean and sober day. In between, stop on the hour and say hello to God. That helps to keep you on track and remind you what you need to be doing.

Resolution

If you do this, I promise that you will have more *peace* in your day!

Gifts

Thought

Once in a while, seemingly out of nowhere, our Higher Power will delight us with something just truly wonderful. We may receive something, there may be a lovely and remarkable coincidence, a divine intervention, a divinely inspired idea, an overwhelmingly tremendous series of events.

These experiences confirm our faith, belief, and trust in God. We marvel at it and know it was a True, transcendentally spiritual contact.

Resolution

These experiences have vital importance and significance in our life. Don't ever be tempted to write it off as just in your head. These are opportunities to strengthen what you have suspected to be true all along. They are beautiful Gifts from above. Smile!

Scott L. Gourson PhD

Breathe

Where there is a breath, there is hope!

CPSIA information can be obtained at www.ICGtesting.com
Printed in the USA
BVOW07*0816270415

396650BV00005B/1/P